Classic
BRITISH CARS

Classic
British Cars

Brian Johnson and Jeff Daniels

Mobilgas

Mobilgas

Mobilgas
SPEC

Mobiloil

Mo
SP

First published in 1999 by Channel 4 Books,
an imprint of Macmillan Publishers Ltd, 25 Eccleston Place, London SW1W 9NF Basingstoke and Oxford.

Associated companies throughout the world.

ISBN 0 7522 1706 2

1 3 5 7 9 10 8 6 4 2

A CIP catalogue record for this book is available from the British Library.

Designed by Robert Updegraff
Printed and bound in Great Britain by Butler & Tanner Ltd, Frome and London
Colour reproduction by Speedscan Ltd, Essex, UK

This book accompanies the television series 'Classic British Cars' made by Uden Associates for Channel 4.
Executive producer: Patrick Uden
Producer/Directors: Tom Adams, James Castle, Johanna Gibbon, Magnus Temple

Title page *The way it was. The young lady driver of the 1958 Twin Cam MGA watches as a smart forecourt attendant fills up her two-seater sports car's tank; customers did not handle the pumps themselves in those days. Her 113mph MG, which new cost £1,265, including £422 purchase tax but excluding the wire wheels which were an optional extra, will return an average 21.8mpg if she does not drive much beyond 80mph. However, with Mobilgas Super premium petrol at around 4s 2d a gallon (just over 20p!), the lady can have the ten-gallon tank filled and still have change from a fiver. The attendant, unasked, will check the oil, topping up if required with summer grade from the bottles held ready in the dispensers. No seat belts, no MOT, no litres and the bill paid in cash: plastic is still a decade and more away.*

CONTENTS

INTRODUCTION

The focus of this book is the classic post-war British car, with an emphasis on the 1960s. In effect, it covers a period during which the British motor industry, having recovered from the war and (in some ways with even more difficulty) from the war's aftermath of austerity, had built itself a position of considerable strength. By 1960, its home market was growing at last to provide a firm foundation for its efforts, and it had become one of Britain's most important exporters. As explained in Chapter 1, its largest company, BMC – the British Motor Corporation – had in addition just been presented with an epoch-making new small car designed by Alec Issigonis, the same man who had been responsible for the much-loved Morris Minor. All it needed was for BMC to take the Mini concept and run with it, to develop it and exploit it in a logical and orderly way, making the most of its great industrial strength (in 1960, apart from its British production centres in Birmingham and Oxford, BMC owned major factories in Australia, Belgium and Spain, and its cars were produced under licence in several other countries). As a second string to its bow, BMC was also able to offer a comprehensive range of sports cars, carrying two of the most respected marque names – MG and Austin-Healey. What is more, BMC was by no means the only British (by which we mean British-owned) company in the industry. There was Jaguar, the Rootes Group, and Standard-Triumph, all based in or near Coventry, and

The Mini was one of the greatest successes of the British motor industry. The sheer timelessness of its design emerges from this 1959 picture: today, forty years on, these smart young models are probably collecting their old-age pensions, but the Mini looks as fresh and familiar as ever. Note, however, that this is an Austin Mini: BMC's fetish for 'badge-engineering' meant the car's early impact was blunted because it was launched as a Morris model as well. But at least they were now calling it the Austin Mini; at launch it was known as the Austin Mini Seven!

Rover (including Land Rover) building cars nearby in Solihull. Between them, these companies offered a huge and diverse range of models including some which have justifiably become seen as classics.

Although this book is called *Classic British Cars*, it is impossible to examine the history of the post-war British motor industry in isolation. The designing and building of cars is a highly competitive business, and to understand why the industry of any one country succeeds – or fails – you have to look at what is happening in other countries and rival industries. This is, perhaps, especially true of the 1960s – a decade that began full of promise for the British manufacturers and ended with them deep in trouble and well on the way to disaster. Part of the reason for that decline was that British managements often failed to appreciate the significance of what was happening in Europe and the USA. It wasn't that they did not look, more that they had a cosy feeling that they knew better. It was an attitude which meant that when in 1945 the British army discovered the ruins of a large factory at Wolfsburg in West Germany, making a strange device called the Volkswagen, a group of British motor industry experts examined the design, pronounced it inferior in most respects and said it would never sell!

This attitude persisted, and quite possibly became more entrenched, during the 1960s. Throughout this book, despite its title, the reader will find references to the more successful car designs to emerge from Europe and the USA during the 1960s. These references try to make it easier to understand where British management got it wrong. There was very little attempt, in those days, to learn from what we now call

Some of the British motor industry's posed publicity shots suggest scenarios which stretch credibility. The message here is presumably that the 2+2 Coupé version of the superb Jaguar E-type would accommodate husband, wife and two standard children and still have room for luggage. But was it necessary to drive the poor thing along a rough track into the middle of a Scottish forest? And are they really going to put those logs in the back? No doubt the E-type, which was practical as well as beautiful, managed to cope ...

The Triumph Herald was a bold attempt to be innovative. It was the last mass-produced British car to have a separate chassis: one advantage was that it was very easy to remove the roof and turn it into a convertible, as seen here. Also, famously, the entire bonnet lifted forwards in one piece to provide superb access to the engine for maintenance and repair. But the fact that this chap is looking slightly less happy – despite the smart young lady beside him – may have something to do with the Herald's handling, which thanks to its swing-axle rear suspension was certainly not one of its better features.

'best practice'. At worst, the British were insular to the point of deliberate blindness, so that in the early 1970s Lord Stokes, the Chairman of British Leyland, could still say that 'anyone who buys a foreign car must be mad'. Yet there was nothing mad about anyone who chose the sheer reliability of the Volkswagen Beetle, the comfort and versatility of a Renault 16, or the sheer driver appeal of an Alfa Romeo Giulia. The British industry of the 1960s could have built rivals to any of these cars, and sometimes it did; not only the Mini but also – for instance – the original Lotus Elan, the Rover and Triumph 2000s, the Jaguar E-type and XJ6, and the Rolls-Royce Silver Shadow.

These were some of the British successes which could hold their own in any foreign company. They were the major classics, if one defines a classic as a design which has stood the test of time and which in one way or another influenced the way other leading designers thought and the way the motor car evolved. Certainly there were other, minor, classics which may not have been quite so influential but which helped to establish the still-admired idea of 'Britishness', of quality-in-depth, yet always deliberately understated: the kind of impression you gained from the earlier Rovers and the better Rootes Group cars, for example.

Yet in a way, and perhaps more so with hindsight, these classics and near-classics betray another British failing: an inability to appreciate just how good some of these cars were and how much potential for development they offered. This was a blindness just as important as the unwillingness to examine and learn from the best of the foreign rivals. The Mini was the most obvious case in point. It was not so much a car as a concept, the design which sold the idea of a transverse engine and front-wheel drive to the whole motoring world, and it cried out for a sensible extension of its principles into an orderly range of cars. Yet BMC, after starting well enough with the much admired and commercially successful 1100/1300 series, created a range that was anything but orderly, as related in Chapter 2. Worse still, lacking the courage of its convictions, it kept a ramshackle collection of conventional rear-drive models in parallel production, long past their final sell-by date. Meanwhile, instead of developing the Mini, BMC became obsessed with replacing it – an obsession from which, some would argue, even Rover's present owners suffer. In any case, it was this attitude of mind which caused BMC, and to some extent the whole of the British industry, to produce not only a good many classic cars but also some real duds, cars which were either too ugly to sell, or simply so lacking in quality or character that the customers didn't want to know. This book is an attempt to place both classics and duds in some kind of context.

The British were certainly not alone in producing duds, and we are certainly not suggesting that they would have done better to imitate slavishly what was being done in Europe. For example, one of the better things the British did was to ignore – with the sole misguided exception of the Hillman Imp – the post-war European enthusiasm for rear-mounted engines (the Volkswagen Beetle succeeded despite its rear engine, not because of it). Another British achievement was to keep the spirit of the sports car alive and well when almost everyone else had lost interest in it (Chapter 3). Yet in the end, even this provided yet another example of how the British could snatch disaster out of triumph by backing the wrong product. Nothing could illustrate this unfortunate gift better than the Rover Group's eventual decision to close the MG factory at Abingdon while still believing anyone could make a storming success of cars like the Morris Ital and the Austin Maestro. Although this final move came much later, the misguidedness and neglect which led in that direction began in the 1960s.

So look at these cars, the British and the foreign. Make up your own mind which British designs were classics – in many cases not developed as they might have been; and which ones were duds, on whose development the effort was simply wasted. Look at the foreign cars and consider which ones would have provided the British with useful pointers, if enough notice had been taken of them. History still has lessons to teach. One of those lessons is that even though, for all kinds of reasons – from trade union intransigence, through weak and short-sighted management to thoroughly misguided government interference – all but a few tiny parts of the British industry eventually ended up in foreign hands, there was no shortage of design and engineering effort, inspiration and sometimes sheer brilliance at work here in the 1960s, producing cars which qualify as classics and which will be admired for decades to come.

CHAPTER ONE

FROM MAJOR TO MINOR

*a*S GROUCHO MARX once memorably remarked: 'If the horse had not been invented, there would have been nothing to replace it . . .' The horse was in time replaced by the 'horseless carriage', which itself was to be continuously replaced on an almost annual basis as technology progressed until, by the mid-1930s, the design of the popular 'family' car was static in the engineering sense. The cars were built down to a price that could be as low as £100 for a very basic 8hp Model Y Ford. With the ruthless competition for the still relatively small family market, 'new' models were offered by British manufacturers every year. However, many of the new cars had only cosmetic changes, just sufficient to make the (say) 1938 Super Ten recognizably different from the 1937 model. This would encourage customers to change their car in order to 'keep up with the Joneses' (although why they felt they needed to do so remains an intriguing social question). In considering that question it should be remembered that ownership of a private car between the wars was the exception rather than, as now, the rule.

In the late 1930s few car owners below the level of senior management used their cars for commuting. An excellent, inexpensive network of municipally owned public transport existed in all cities and towns, with either tramcar, trolley bus or the newly introduced diesel-engined bus services available on what today would be considered a lavish scale. The average family car before the war thus became more of a status symbol than, as it is today, an essential means of everyday transport. In the 1930s, car ownership was irrelevant to the scale of public transport allocation whereas nowadays the opposite is the case, particularly in rural areas. In 1938, the cost of a tram ticket for a white-collar worker, from the newly built outer suburbs of Liverpool (the areas of car-owning commuters) to the city centre (about 8 miles), was only 3d (just over

A 1965 'Highlight' Minor 1000 with the 'slatted' grille and undivided curved windscreen. This four-door saloon had the 1098cc engine as standard which was able to compensate for the additional weight of the two extra doors, which had starkly revealed a serious shortage of power available from the 918cc engines of the early four-door Minor saloons and commercial vans.

Piccadilly Circus c. 1944. The lack of any petrol for private motoring is reflected in this wartime photograph. There are no private cars visible at all; only taxis, buses, two commercial vans and a horse-drawn van behind the boarded-up plinth of Eros (the statue was removed for safety during the war years). The original print reveals the famous flower seller on the Eros steps, and that among the civilian pedestrians are many service men and women braving the constant threat of the German V1 'Doodle Bug' pilotless flying bombs and the later V2 rockets when in search of entertainment in London.

1p) or $2\frac{1}{2}$p return per day. For the equivalent of 3p (7d) his wife could buy an 'all-day' ticket offering unlimited journeys for shopping in the city centre. Even allowing for inflation, pre-war urban transport costs were low: a white-collar worker in 1938 would spend roughly a twentieth of his disposable income on travelling to work by public transport (a woman would spend rather more; her fares would remain the same but women – for example, teachers – were paid substantially less than their male colleagues).

In 1938 many people still lived and worked in the same town; the 8 miles a Liverpool commuter had to travel each day would be about the maximum outside London. Today, a direct comparison is difficult as social and environmental changes have required commuters to travel far greater distances. Many people live in one town but work in another, the consequence being that a far higher proportion of disposable income is now spent on commuting. With the high cost, and often diminished and erratic service, of public transport, it is small wonder that many use a car in order to travel to work. In 1938, however, most family cars, summer holidays apart, remained in the garage throughout the week. On Saturday they were washed and polished (and seen by the neighbours), before the Sunday afternoon 'run' with the family. Of course, then as now, there was a stratification of ownership: the Morris Eight man deferred to the Rover Twelve owner, though he felt himself superior to the driver of a Model Y Ford.

The Second World War ended all domestic car production. The major manufacturers were producing either army vehicles, such as trucks and tanks, or aircraft, and the smaller 'independents' were contracted to do precision machining work, mainly for the aircraft industry. Although 'war work' was the official business of the industry at that time, several designers were informally discussing (often to relieve the tedium of the compulsory night-long fire-watching duties in factories) the shape and nature of the post-war car. One, a young member of the Morris Motors design staff, Alec Issigonis, knew exactly what kind of post-war car he would design given the chance. Eventually, as we shall see, he was provided with the opportunity in 1948. The car he designed was destined to become a true classic: the Morris Minor. This was a design that was truly original, and which advanced the technology of the family car.

Fifteen years on and Piccadilly Circus presents a very different scene. Crowds surround the returned Eros statue, private cars dominate the traffic, CinZano and lager have replaced wartime Bovril, and Dunlop tyres, unobtainable during the war years, have displaced the famous advertment for Wrigley's chewing gum. With petrol at around 4s a gallon (40p) even the owner of the 1960 3.4 Jaguar can enjoy carefree motoring on the newly opened motorways.

THE LIGHTWEIGHT SPECIAL

From 1937 Issigonis had been working on a proposal for an independent front-suspension system for the 1938 Morris Series M Ten. Independent front suspension (ifs) was, in the late 1930s, considered to be a major selling-point for small cars, replacing the almost universal beam axle and cart-springing which, in essentials, had remained unchanged for some forty years.

The system Issigonis was developing was the now familiar coil spring and wishbone with hydraulic shock absorbers, linked to light and precise rack-and-pinion steering. In the event, the M Series Morris was built with a conventional, cheaper, beam front-axle and the ifs work was shelved (it was to reappear with the 1.25-litre MG saloon introduced in May 1947).

Issigonis had also, with a like-minded friend, J.M.P. 'George' Dowson, designed and built by hand, before the war, a remarkable single-seat hill-climb and sprint car that they had named the 'Lightweight Special'. It was indeed lightweight, for weight-saving had been the main remit of the design. Based on a pre-war supercharged 747cc Austin Seven Ulster engine and running gear, the Lightweight Special had a stunning *monoposto* aluminium body that might have been inspired by the 1937 Mercedes W-125 Grand Prix cars – then proving to be almost unbeatable.

The Lightweight's elegant body had an integral box section and the whole was load-bearing because of its stressed-skin monocoque construction, at that time a form of construction normally reserved for advanced fighter aircraft. The beautifully made bodyshell concealed the most enterprising aspects of the car, for the suspension was independent on all four wheels. The front-wheel suspension was by short double wishbones with bell cranks on the top, which compressed rubber within a transverse tube. At the rear was an independent swing-axle arrangement with a number of aero-rubber shock cords in tension, suspending the two driven half-axles. The differential and four-speed gearbox were standard Austin Ulster components. To reduce the unsprung weight, all four wheels were cast in a light alloy with integral brake drums. The supercharged 747cc Austin engine and the low weight of the car (around 700lb) made it unbeatable in its class. The Lightweight was laid up during the war years, fortunately surviving the many wartime 'scrap-metal drives' which needlessly claimed many interesting pre-war cars.

After the war, Issigonis and Dowson revised the Lightweight, fitting an experimental Morris Zoller supercharged overhead camshaft (ohc) engine of only 748cc, which nevertheless developed 95bhp and gave the car, weighing in at 720lb, a speed of 110mph at the early post-war club meetings. Issigonis and Dowson entered and drove the Lightweight Special for three years in club events where the car was proved once again to be all but unbeatable. Issigonis eventually felt that the pressures of the day job were becoming too great and the car was, reluctantly, sold. (Happily, the Lightweight still exists and is raced in suitable Vintage Sports Car Club – VSCC –

Sir Alec Issigonis seemed unable to hold a conversation without a pencil or pen in his hand, sketching original ideas and projects on anything to hand, be it a restaurant tablecloth, the back of an envelope or the sheets of paper he used by the ream when, as here, in his Longbridge office.

events.) Alec Issigonis, then aged fifty-six, drove the car at a club meeting at Oulton Park in 1962, with George Dowson still fit enough to push-start the car. Although the Lightweight was sold Issigonis had probably learned all he could from the car. They were proved to be extremely valuable lessons.

In September 1939, with the change from civil to war production, Issigonis was engaged as project engineer at Morris Motors involved in design work on armoured cars and an amphibious tracked armoured fighting vehicle (AFV). The war work, however essential, was far removed from Issigonis's passion: the innovative design of small cars.

THE MOSQUITO

Despite the factory where Morris cars were made being fully committed to war production, Miles (later Sir Miles) Thomas, the newly appointed managing director and vice-chairman of what had then become the Nuffield Organization, briefed Issigonis in 1942 to design and construct, as a working prototype, a four-seat 'ideas car'. This would now be termed a 'concept' car, where a talented designer is given a free hand to put forward future ideas, which are not constrained by costing or current production techniques but which, nevertheless, advance the styling and/or technology of automotive design. This prototype was to be worked on with a view to possible production in the post-war family car market. Apart from assuming that the UK would win that war, Miles Thomas had correctly foreseen that petrol rationing, which was rigidly enforced during the war years, would not immediately be restored for private motoring as soon as the war was over. Therefore a small, frugal car was likely to prove more popular than a large, thirsty one. Thomas also correctly foresaw that the existing 1939 Morris Eight, which it was then assumed would resume production once the war was over, was already dated and in urgent need of replacement.

Issigonis, together with two draftsmen, Jack Daniels and Reg Job, set to work and proposed a compact car with curved body lines, tentatively named 'Mosquito'. This proposal would fit Miles Thomas's low petrol consumption requirements as the engine would only displace less than 1 litre (800cc). The small saloon represented a technological advance on the Morris Eight it would replace as it was, in many ways, representative of the quintessence of Issigonis's thinking: an original design, and free (for the moment) from the constraints of the boardroom and accountants. All the accumulated experience gained from racing the Lightweight Special and the received knowledge of the work done by innovative designers in the USA contributed to Issigonis's design. The resultant Mosquito therefore had an 'airflow' body shape and independent front suspension, both being a departure from any existing pre-war British family car. It remains an important landmark because it was, in effect, the prototype of the post-war Morris Minor.

Alec Issigonis was never a man merely to copy other designs, but that does not mean that he would not use such work as a reference if it suited his vision of the small car of the future. Therefore the Mosquito, as Issigonis freely acknowledged, owed a good deal in its body styling to the influence of the rounded panels of American cars of the late 1930s. These were pioneered by Carl Breer's 1935 Chrysler and De Soto 'airflow' body shapes, which had influenced the stylists of Chevrolet, Plymouth and other US manufacturers. This 'streamforming', as it was originally termed – soon to be changed to 'streamlining' – became an almost universal icon from the mid-1930s to the early 1940s in the USA. It had begun with monoplane passenger aircraft, such as the Douglas DC-2, spreading to cars, railway locomotives, domestic refrigerators, radios and other everyday domestic equipment, as imaginative US designers, led by Carl Breer, Raymond Loewy and Norman Bel Geddes, utilized new, improved and cost-effective steel-panel stamping and die-casting techniques. These permitted the mass production of flowing curves and smooth shapes. In the USA, the latest streamlined cars, railroad trains, furniture and domestic artefacts that appeared in Hollywood films also no doubt helped to make the transition from the dated square and upright forms to the new popular, 'modern' idiom. It was to take longer for streamlining to gain full acceptance in Europe because the turnover of cars and domestic appliances, to say nothing of the rolling-stock on the railways, was far slower. The European public were also less susceptible to advertising because, at the time, there were no concentrated commercial radio and, later, television campaigns. Americans, from the mid-1930s onwards, tended to regard domestic possessions – including cars – as transitory, regularly to be replaced by newer, up-to-date, and therefore by definition, better, products.

However, under the Mosquito's shapely American-inspired bodyshell, the running gear devised by Issigonis owed nothing to contemporary Detroit practice. The Mosquito's body was of an integral construction, with no separate chassis. A separate chassis was, in the 1940s, still universal in the USA. In addition, in place of the soft coil-springing favoured by American designers – the better to iron out the rough dirt roads common in rural states and offering a smooth ride at the expense of vague steering, excessive body roll and poor road-holding at speed – the Mosquito had precise light rack-and-pinion steering and front torsion-bar independent suspension, both borrowed from that of the trend-setting French Citroën Light 15 *Traction Avant.* (This had been devised in 1934 by some of the best designers in the field, and was the favoured vehicle of the French Gendarmerie.)

Torsion-bar suspension basically consists of a steel rod that is loaded by twisting it with one end fixed, the other free end connected to the suspension linkage of the front wheels. The problem is that a very high grade of steel is required to combat the inevitable fatigue failure induced by endless stress reversals. Issigonis knew that the commercially available steel torsion bars were very expensive, so the small design team decided to make their own 'in-house'. The final body shape, steering and suspension of the prototype Mosquito had been settled by 1943. Issigonis had wanted to have all-round independent suspension via torsion bars but, mainly on grounds of costing, the proposal for rear-wheel independent suspension never got beyond the design stage. Instead, conventional semi-elliptical springs with seven leaves were fitted. Front-wheel drive had also been considered but that too had been abandoned largely on grounds of cost although, later, Issigonis admitted that he had not been certain he knew how to do it. The question of the engine remained to be finalized.

For the Mosquito, Issigonis had designed a new 'flat-four' engine. The flat-four engine, with twin horizontally opposed pistons, was a type much favoured as a power plant for light aircraft. It had several merits, one of which was the low height of the engine, which then lowered the car's centre of gravity. All in all, Issigonis had considered it to be the best option for the car. Because the design philosophy of the body included a compact flat-four engine envisaged as the powerplant, there was hence a very wide engine compartment. The proposed engine was to be available in two capacities: 800cc for the home market, and with the cylinders bored out to 1,100cc for export. Both sizes, however, were to have side valves. This rather retrograde step was, to some extent, forced on Issigonis by the width of the car. The wide horizontal engine had to fit between the front-wheel arches, as the additional engine bay width needed to accommodate the rocker boxes of an overhead valve engine was too great. That was not the only problem. From the start there had been opposition to the flat-four engine. Lord Nuffield (the former William Morris and still chairman of the company he had founded in 1913) personally was firmly against it but Issigonis argued that the flat-four engine was a major part of the design philosophy of the car and, as the designer, his primary choice. Although the engine had been designed in detail by Issigonis it was actually to be built at the Nuffield engine factory at Courthouse Green, Coventry. The chief engineer at the Coventry works, Tom Brown, did not want to build the Issigonis flat-four engine, possibly because of the well-known wartime boffin's syndrome of 'NIH' (Not Invented Here)! However, Issigonis may have got Miles Thomas to pull rank, for a prototype engine, or to be accurate engines – for at least two prototypes, one engine of each capacity – are known to have been built at Coventry. One of the, ultimately eight, Mosquito prototypes was certainly powered by an Issigonis 800cc flat-four in April 1947. It was not a success. Against all expectation the engine had appalling vibration. Jack Daniels was later to claim that the Coventry engine works had deliberately ignored the drawings and had used an incorrect method of bolting the flywheel to the crankshaft, which had caused the atypical vibration (they had omitted the locating dowels). It was also reported by Tom Brown that on the evidence of test-running on the bench at Courthouse Green, the 800cc engine lacked sufficient torque for the three-speed gearbox Issigonis had also proposed for the Mosquito. There were, in addition, allegations from Coventry that the crankshaft and bearings were of unsatisfactory design. Whatever the true reasons, the fact was that the flat-four engine was abandoned. Issigonis then suggested, as an alternative, that the overhead-valve 918cc Wolseley engine be used in the Mosquito. Lord Nuffield vetoed that: he favoured the mechanical simplicity of side-valve engines (strangely, Lord Nuffield retained the prototype Wolseley Eight with overhead valves as his personal transport from 1939 to 1955).

It was now 1946, the war was over and there was a demand for new cars. The existing stock of pre-1939 cars had mostly been 'laid up' – unused during the war years due to their owners being in the services or, if not in the services, unable to qualify for a petrol allowance as all 'pleasure' motoring was forbidden (only 'essential' users, such as doctors and those whose war work required the use of a car, were allowed petrol – though some users, it has to be said, were more 'essential' than others'). Many of the unused cars deteriorated in damp garages, many more were lost or damaged in air raids, some had been requisitioned and all were six, or more, years old and thus dated. Young ex-servicemen who had flown four-engined bombers or high-speed fighters and advanced armoured fighting vehicles and who had the advantage of service gratuity money wanted something better. Hollywood films presented the latest American designs and fashions, which had continued to be available in the USA despite the war. Major social changes also had a powerful influence: Churchill had been dismissed from power – perhaps partly due to the sergeants of the Army Bureau of Current Affairs (ABCA) lecturing soldiers about to be demobilized on the merits of socialism and the need for a Labour government.

In order to meet the expected demand for new cars all the major pre-war manufacturers prepared to convert their production lines from war work back to civilian motor cars. Most production planned for the civil market was of an interim nature being, in the main, shelved 1939 designs. Morris was no exception and the pre-war Eight, with cosmetic changes, was soon back in production, to be followed by the completely new Issigonis Mosquito. In order to get this car into production a decision was needed about the engine. To save time, Issigonis had little alternative but to agree to use the very moderate 919cc 27bhp side-valve engine (a flathead in the USA) designed before the war. These were fitted to the Morris Eight Series E saloons, which were by then in full production. It was a smooth-running, reliable and well-proved motor, but lacked power. However, the question of the engine was not the only urgent problem Issigonis was to face in getting his Mosquito concept into production . . .

When Lord Nuffield was shown the prototype Mosquito, he took one look and then commented that it looked 'like a poached egg'. He liked his Morris cars to have, in addition to a side-valve engine, a conventional radiator and bonnet; he disliked the shape and he disliked the name Mosquito. He also disliked Issigonis, only once speaking directly to him, never mentioning him by name, and always referring to the designer as 'that foreign chap'. (Alec Issigonis, although British, had been born of naturalized parents in Smyrna.) Finally, and most damning, Lord Nuffield did not think that there was any need for the car at all as the Series E Morris Eight was selling as fast as it could be built. However, it was selling because there was a desperate shortage of any new cars and although the Eight was basically a pre-war design with a distinctly moderate performance, it *was* available. In the light of Lord Nuffield's views, the management dithered; at one point it was suggested that perhaps Lord Nuffield was right and the whole Mosquito project should be dropped.

1947: the year of austerity with practically everything either unobtainable or in short supply. The meagre 'basic' petrol ration grudgingly permitted for 'pleasure' motoring in the euphoria following the end of the war had been withdrawn. Enraged motorists were asked to attend a protest rally for, as the placards on this battered pre-war saloon point out, the defeated Germans had an allowance of 180 miles a month while the British, the victors, now had nothing. The protest failed: few it seemed had sufficient petrol to get to the Hyde Park rally.

THE BIRTH OF THE MORRIS MINOR

Miles Thomas rejected the proposal to abandon the Mosquito; he knew that if the Nuffield company was to survive in the longer term, a technically advanced and up-to-date 'modern' design was essential. The pre-war German Volkswagen Beetle, the French front-wheel drive Citroëns and the Italian Fiats and Lancias were all much more advanced cars than the beam axle and cart-sprung Morris Eight, even though it was a venerable design. Thomas clearly saw that once the first flush of buying by a car-starved public was over and the war-damaged European factories got fully under way, competition would be fierce. Miles Thomas managed to convince a sceptical Lord Nuffield that European competition was only a matter of time and also used the argument that the new Issigonis car would be cheaper to produce and sell than the existing Morris Eight (it is doubtful if he really believed that to be true). Astutely, he then suggested that the name Mosquito should be changed. He knew Nuffield disliked it and that many people – especially ex-servicemen – associated it with either malaria or the very fast wartime RAF's De Havilland Mosquito bomber. He suggested instead the name 'Morris Minor' in tribute to the successful £100 Minor of 1931,

which had allowed the Morris company successfully to challenge Herbert Austin's famous 'Seven'. That turned the argument and in 1948, two years late, Lord Nuffield reluctantly consented to put the new Morris Minor, as designed by 'that foreign chap', into full-scale production at the Cowley, Oxford works of Morris Motors.

The aim was to get the new Series MM Morris Minor into production in time to be unveiled at the October 1948 London Motor Show, the first to be held for ten years. Long lead items were bought and held in the stores, and dies, jigs and tools were ordered and fitted to the production lines. All was ready when Issigonis called for a halt. He had decided, on aesthetic grounds alone, after driving the prototype and spending some time just walking round and round it, that the car was too narrow. Production Minors had to be made 4in wider, an increase from 4ft 9in to 5ft 1in. The Nuffield board were persuaded that the wider body, which of course increased the passenger compartment space, would not cost any more to produce than the original narrower body. How Issigonis managed to sort out the problem of the cost of the expensive replacement body-pressing tools and jigs remains unknown. The change was accepted by the board – did they conceal it from Lord Nuffield? There remained however, a local difficulty: the Cowley stores held a large quantity of Minor front and rear bumpers which were now 4in too short. They were neatly cut in two and fitted to the early production cars with a riveted 4in distance piece in the middle, through which the front ones accommodated that now vanished but useful accessory, the starting handle. (The stores must have held a very large number of those short bumpers for it was not until 1951, by which time 48,000 Minors had been produced, that the split bumpers finally disappeared.)

The Motor Show of October 1948 was a sell-out; over half a million people visited the exhibition. Many were ex-servicemen, too young to hold a licence before the war but who had learned to drive Jeeps and trucks in the forces, and who were now eager to buy their first car. It is difficult, now, to realize the conditions of life in the Britain of 1948. The debilitating war had dragged on for six years with rationing, a total blackout (that is, no light of any description visible from the air), rigidly enforced shortages of practically everything, long hours working in factories or offices without adequate heating, air raids, or the fear of them made worse by the 1944 V2 rockets and V1 flying bombs, and the war continuing on many fronts beyond the seas. When peace had arrived in 1945 there was a brief euphoria when people realized that they had survived the war years, and then a sense that they had been promised a false future. The ideals of a 'better world' were not being fulfilled. There was the most severe winter for years; fuel shortages; continuing food rationing – indeed, if anything, worse than during the war with bread being rationed for the first time; and clothing also rationed by 'clothing coupons'. There was an air of overall utility, austerity and drabness without the imperative of waging a war perceived to be just. Demobilized servicemen felt betrayed and resentful. Then, in 1948, there was a small fashion miracle: the 'New Look' imported from France. The New Look enabled young women to discard the drab wartime uni-

Opposite *An early Morris Minor Tourer. Indeed NWL 433, photographed in Banbury in 1948, could well be a pre-production prototype: its registration was issued before NWL 576* (overleaf), *known to be the first production Minor. The tourer displays the identification features of the early cars: 'low-light' headlamps; divided windscreen; 'cheese grater' radiator grille; and the added distance piece to widen the bumper when Issigonis decided to increase the width of the Minors after a large number of bumpers had been delivered. The two young ladies were probably from the BMC press office. Today that car would be very valuable: tourers are the rarest of Minors as so few were made; surviving cars are much sought after to the extent that Minor saloons are cut up as fake tourers.*

NWL 576 was the first production Morris Minor; the car was retained by the company and fully restored by apprentices as part of the celebration marking the production of the one-millionth Minor in 1961. Note the 'low-light' head lamps and divided windscreen with single wiper; also visible is the 'semaphore' trafficator just behind the shut line of the single door, and the bumper widening piece.

forms and civilian clothing, and both look and feel feminine and glamorous. It was as if a monochrome world had suddenly become full of bright colour. At last, it was felt, the war was over. As with clothes, so with cars. The thousands who thronged to the London Motor Show were eager to see the brightly painted cars of their future, not mere cosmetic workovers of the pre-war designs, most of which were available only in black.

It's got what it takes to make a small car **BIG**

The "Quality first" MORRIS MINOR is a good looking small car. Conceived with no concessions to compromise it is a BIG CAR scaled down. There is no other small car anywhere in the world that has so many BIG CAR refinements as the MORRIS MINOR.

Styling inside and out is modern and impressive ; independent front suspension by torsion bars—the greatest single advance in modern car design, provides smooth tireless travel on the longest journey ; steering is light and positive ; seats are deep and wide and there is plenty of head and leg room.

The MORRIS MINOR is easy to park in a small space and steer through traffic ; less costly to maintain ; economical to buy and to run. *No wonder it is the most sought after small car in the world.*

The Morris Minor saloons on display were the New Look of the car industry, and were the most modern cars in the show; the perfect proportions and well-blended curves gave just the right impression of being excitingly 'new' and vaguely transatlantic. The two headlamps were recessed low down into the front wings and the 14in (slightly smaller than standard) wheels gave the car a low 'four-square' appearance, which hinted at the excellent road-holding the cars in fact possessed. There was also a long front bench seat, as seen in American films, roomy passenger space and the cars came in a range of bright colours. All these things were new to British car buyers.

The trade papers gave the Morris Minor a very good press. The influential *Motor* described the car as the 'Show sensation' which, considering that another new car, the Jaguar XK 120, was also making its début, was praise indeed. *The Autocar*'s reviewer was impressed by the Minor's styling and called it 'a triumph in good looks'. Road test reports praised the car's handling and fuel economy of up to 40mpg – an important matter, as petrol rationing was still in force, and a point that had been emphasized in the company's pre-show publicity. *The Autocar* had a line drawing in their show report depicting a Minor almost submerged by eager visitors to the Nuffield stand. The price of the MM two-door Minor Saloon, the only option then available, was announced as £359.

The stressing of fuel economy in the company literature was not altogether a consequence of petrol rationing. The simple truth was that the Minor, though admittedly all that could have been hoped for in the matter of road-holding and styling was, it was whispered, a little underpowered. By the standards of today it certainly was: 0–60mph in 55 seconds with a maximum of 62mph. The Minor was no ball of fire but it should be remembered that in 1948 there was only a meagre 'basic' petrol ration, so motorists tended to drive with extreme economy in mind. The average speed of main road traffic was still around the pre-war figure of 45mph; there were no motorways, and few dual-carriage roads. Only a number of sports cars could exceed 80mph. High speeds were simply not important in the conditions of 1948; just to drive a car, any car, was almost a sufficient end in itself. So few of the eager buyers of the Minors complained about performance, the lack of which became apparent to the factory in 1950 with, firstly, the testing of the prototype four-door Minor saloon and, secondly and starkly, with the road trials of the prototype 5cwt Morris Minor van. The four-door saloon, with the additional weight of the extra two doors (about ½cwt) drastically reduced the just-adequate performance available with the two-door car. The situation with the commercial van, on which large fleet orders from the Post Office were in prospect, was desperate; the performance was quite unacceptable and vans were expected to account for up to 20 per cent of the total Minor production. The inescapable conclusion was clear: 27.5bhp was simply not sufficient. The engine question was once again on the agenda.

The Nuffield board decided to power all future Minor vans and four-door saloons with the 33bhp Wolseley-based overhead valve (ohv) engine that Alec Issigonis had wanted as the alternative to his rejected flat-four two years previously. Unfortunately, the Wolseley engine and the car that it powered were both now out of production; there were difficulties in getting it back into production, due to tooling problems, caused by the inability of the toolmakers to guarantee a delivery date for a vital cylinder-block-transfer machine before January 1953. That was, in part, because of the Korean War and the consequent government rearmament orders having priority for precision machine tools. Another delay was the adoption of imperial (SAE) threads in the revised engine. Curiously, the Morris and Wolseley engines had metric threads at a time when most British cars used imperial standards. This anomaly on the part of Morris Motors was a historical legacy dating from the French-designed Hotchkiss engines, which had been built under licence at Cowley to power the original 'Bullnose' Morris Oxfords of the 1920s.

By July 1951, with the tooling difficulties resolved, the Nuffield board was assured that the delayed full-scale production of the 33hp, rather dated, ex-Wolseley engine could commence by January 1952. The matter was now urgent as the new rival Austin A30, with an 803cc overhead-valve engine, an obvious competitor to the Minor, was announced at the 1951 London Motor Show and had been well received by press and public. A Nuffield board meeting was held on 30 October 1951, just after the Motor Show. The minutes noted that: 'It was agreed that in spite of the advent of the new Austin Seven [A30] no anxiety need be entertained regarding the future of the Morris Minor . . . [but] it was thought to be of the first importance to do everything to expedite the introduction of the ohv [Wolseley] engine . . .'

There were no more Nuffield board meetings after that date for the very simple reason that there was no longer any Nuffield board, or indeed any Morris Motors. The Austin Motor Company, for more than thirty years their arch-competitor, had taken over the Nuffield Organization to form the British Motor Corporation (BMC), which was to become one of the largest European producers of motor vehicles; economies of

Opposite *In an era when black and white commercial television concentrated on selling detergents, toothpaste and baked beans, the motor trade relied on colour printed advertisements to promote their products. This excellent artwork for a Minor saloon of the 1960s stresses that despite the name 'Minor' the car has '. . . got what it takes to make a small car big'. The typically middle-class family depicted are extolling the safety and the room of the car and even discuss the virtues of engine accessibility, hydraulic brakes and the torsion arm suspension, an indication of the growing awareness of the importance of technology among prospective buyers in the highly competitive market of the 1960s.*

scale were apparent by this time. The new chief was a very competitive man: Leonard Lord, a brilliant ex-production engineer who had spent most of his working life in the industry to become the head of Austin Motors, and who now was the head of BMC.

By August 1952 Lord resolved the question of a more powerful engine for the four-door Minor saloon, to be known as the Series II Saloon, and for the Minor vans. This was the enforced use of the engine, clutch and four-speed gearbox of the markedly inferior powerplant of the Austin A30. This was an 803cc-unit overhead-valve engine which, though smaller in capacity than the original Morris unit, did offer a marginal increase in performance. The perceptive motoring journalist John Bolster, writing in *The Autosport*, said of the Austin-powered Minor: '. . . but as this [Austin 803cc engine] is appreciably smaller than the old one, it is not very much faster. Furthermore, the gearbox that goes with the new motor is not as pleasant as the original.' Moreover, the use of the Austin engine cast a depressing shadow over the Morris engine factory at Coventry which had, to a large extent, been sidelined. If they had not so peremptorily dumped the Issigonis flat-four engine they would have been in a much stronger position. Experienced Morris personnel thought that the Austin package was not up to the engineering standards of the Morris units. The Austin engine and running gear were much more lightly built and the gearbox, as John Bolster had noted, was not as smooth to operate. The Morris units tended to be over-engineered, the foundry techniques being based on pre-war alloys which required a much thicker wall than the post-war metals; these more modern metals were the result of wartime aviation experience. The result was that, by comparison, Morris-built engines and gearboxes were much more silent and durable than the newer, more powerful Austin equivalents.

The reliability of the side-valve engine was such that these early Minors began to appear on the second-hand market. A growing number of club-racing enthusiasts bought them and, wishing to exploit the excellent road-holding abilities of the Series MM Minor, began to tune the engines for more power. Before long, commercial kits were made available to convert the sluggish side-valve engine into an overhead-valve version. Among the proprietary ohv conversion kits, the best-known was the Alta, which came from a well-known company that had been producing excellent four-cylinder ohc engines for the Formula II, Grand Prix Connaught, Cooper-Alta and the HWM, with which the young Stirling Moss made his entry into serious European Grand Prix competition. The Morris Minor Alta DIY conversion kit was not quite in that league but, costing – in 1954 – the relatively small sum of £43 10s, it converted the standard side-valve 27hp Morris MM saloon into quite a competitive 38hp ohv sports car. John Bolster, reporting on an *Autosport* road test run on an Alta-converted Minor, gave a maximum speed of 78mph and 0–60 in 20.4 seconds. Bolster noted that the Minor's speedometer was reading 86mph on the maximum speed run! Optimistic speedometer or not, it was, as Bolster commented, an impressive performance from a 919cc-engined saloon with three people on board. The rather more staid *Motor* magazine, when testing the Alta conversion, merely noted that the ohv engine was more economical when driven hard, compared with its original side-valve performance.

Their tester achieved over 30mpg on average. John Bolster, a perceptive critic of road-holding, having built and raced cars both before and after the war, was fulsome in his praise of the Minor's handling with the uprated engine: 'The performance is improved out of all recognition, and I was at last able to make use of that outstanding road holding . . . the incredulity on the faces of some of the people I passed had to be seen to be believed.' No doubt!

From October 1950, for the more prosaic production Minors, the headlights were moved out of the recesses to a position on the top of the wings to comply with Californian lighting regulations. Issigonis had opposed the change but there was a growing export market for the Minor in America, and it was not considered large enough to make it worthwhile tooling a separate export version. Therefore all Minors from that date onwards had raised lights; the old original Series MM Minors, of which 176,002 had been built, are now referred to as 'low-light' Minors. (It is an interesting commentary on the efficiency of the Issigonis design that the raising of the headlights reduced the maximum speed by 1.2mph.) From January 1953 all Minors had the Austin 803cc ohv engine fitted as standard, and in May that year the long-delayed Minor vans and pick-ups appeared. These led to the 'Traveller', based

A 1000 Mini Traveller, the very popular utility, was first introduced as a Series II in October 1953, with the divided windscreen and the 803cc engine. The 1962 Traveller which superseded it had the 'slatted grille' and the more powerful 1098cc engine. This can be considered the definitive Traveller, much sought-after today, though the ash frame is notoriously prone to rot if not regularly maintained.

A page from the 1953 Mini catalogue which introduced the Mini Traveller. 'You get all the advantages of owning two vehicles' claimed the copy writer – this because the Traveller was developed from the 5cwt Mini van. As usual, the excellent artwork showed a happy family loading the Traveller for their summer holiday. Again, technical details were emphasized: the suspension; instruments (not a strong point with any Mini); the ohv engine with 'its amazing fuel consumption' (this point to explain the rather underpowered performance of the early Travellers). 'For Town and Country for Work and Pleasure' concluded the man from the agency, and that was a fair enough summary. Very few of the original Series II Travellers have survived with the 803cc engine; most have been re-engined with the more powerful later units. Surviving Series IIs in their original state are very rare. Any Mini Traveller in good condition is today very expensive.

For Town and Country – for Work and Pleasure

With their trim smart lines, attractive range of body colours with harmonising upholstery, wide, comfortable seats, and high performance engines, these versatile Travellers Cars are suitable for any and every occasion. Whether you are making a social call, visiting the club, or spending a week-end with friends, a Travellers Car always looks "right." The new, unique MORRIS MINOR TRAVELLERS CAR has most of the fine engineering features of the famous Saloon— superb torsion bar independent front wheel suspension, light, responsive direct-acting steering, a four-speed gearbox, safe positive hydraulic brakes, plus the new overhead valve engine with its amazing performance and fuel economy. Ask for prices. You will be surprised to learn how little it costs to own a MORRIS TRAVELLERS CAR.

EVERYTHING THE TRAVELLER MAY NEED during a long vacation can easily be stowed in the capacious body. A roof lamp is provided for easy loading or unloading at night. A full-length roof liner panel and adequate ventilation protect the interior from the heat of the day.

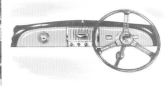

RIDE ON AN EVEN KEEL ON THE ROUGHEST ROAD

FIRM, RESILIENT SUSPENSION keeps the ride steady and level when travelling at speed over rough-surfaced roads. The car is kept on an even keel, road shock and vibration are absorbed. Driver and passengers are free from sway.

INDEPENDENT FRONT SUSPENSION by long torsion bars operating in conjunction with hydraulic dampers, achieves splendid road-holding qualities. The direct-acting steering is remarkably light and positive.

A LIGHT PRESSURE of the fingers is sufficient to slide forward the large side windows. The interior of the car is always cool and fresh. And with this type of ventilation the car is so much safer for children.

PARKING IS EASY because the direct steering is light and responsive.

INSTRUMENTS ARE EDGE-LIGHTED for easy reading by night. Included on the panel is a headlamp beam warning light. (Minor illustrated.)

YOU GET ALL THE ADVANTAGES OF OWNING TWO TYPES OF VEHICLES

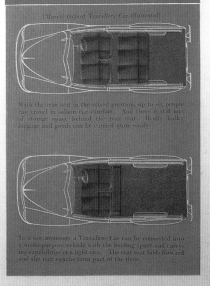

(Morris Oxford Travellers Car illustrated)

With the rear seat in the raised position, up to six people can travel in saloon car comfort. And there is still lots of storage space behind the rear seat. Really bulky luggage and goods can be carried quite easily.

In a few moments a Travellers Car can be converted into a multi-purpose vehicle with the loading space and carrying capabilities of a light van. The rear seat folds forward and the rear squabs form part of the floor.

THE POWER UNIT of the Morris Minor Travellers Car, an overhead valve engine developing 30 b.h.p., gives brisk acceleration and an excellent cruising speed, with amazing fuel economy. The side-valve engine fitted to the Morris Oxford Travellers Car develops 41 b.h.p. This high performance engine has proved its reliability all over the world.

on the American Ford 'woodie', which was then very popular. In the UK such body-work was called an 'estate car' or a 'shooting brake'; BMC were wise to stick to Traveller. Unlike the American Ford Mercury and other woodies, which had a wooden body from the scuttle back, the Traveller had metal panels with ash frames (forty-two pieces, and all of them notoriously prone to rot if not well maintained). The carrying capacity of the Traveller was the same as that of the 5cwt van. In that year, 1953, de-luxe versions of all Minor cars were offered; these had a heater as standard, seats covered with leather, revised bumpers and a sun visor for the passenger.

These later changes to the Minor were made in the absence of the original creator of the car. Alec Issigonis had been lured away from BMC to the old Coventry-based firm of Alvis. The offer was made as he was working on a transverse engine/front-wheel-drive version of the Minor. That work was left incomplete, as the offer from Alvis promised him a free hand and a blank sheet of paper on which to design a brand-new high-performance 3.5-litre V8-engined luxury saloon car, aimed at a very different market from the Minor. The projected Alvis bristled with innovative Issigonis features including an unorthodox gearbox with a built-in unit with the differential, a feature usually only found on contemporary Grand Prix cars. The design also incorporated a revolutionary form of rubber suspension; this was a developed version of the rather crude, though successful, system pioneered on the pre-war Lightweight Special. For the suspension, Alec Issigonis was working in close collaboration with Alex Moulton, now remembered mainly for his revolutionary bicycles. Issigonis and Moulton had proposed a suspension for the Alvis that consisted of a rubber/fluid system with interconnections between the front and rear wheels. This 'levelled' the car on rough roads, and was a system that was ultimately to appear on the BMC 1100/1300s. Sadly, despite the excellent promise of the design, the Alvis company joined the many famous and old-established names that were, by the end of the 1950s, in serious financial difficulties. The Issigonis V8 Alvis remained a paper proposal, not even a prototype being built; it remains a tantalizing prospect of what might have been.

After the disappointing termination of the Alvis project, Leonard Lord offered Issigonis the post of chief engineer at BMC in 1955, with the remit of designing original cars for future production. The Minor was, of course, still in full production. That same year was to see sales of no fewer than 88,733 Minors of all types. Against this satisfactory background, Issigonis, heading a small, devoted design team with a workshop and design office at Longbridge, began to create forward-looking projects, all of which incorporated Issigonis's original thinking. The first project was a 1.5-litre saloon that utilized the now patented Moulton 'Hydrolastic' rubber/fluid suspension. This had been evolved for the stillborn Alvis V8. The BMC concept (coded XC 9001) never got beyond a running prototype. However, the next proposal, XC 9002, a similar though smaller car that was seen as a possible replacement for the Minor became, in the event, the basis of the successful Morris 1100.

Whatever the project under design development, Alec Issigonis was very much a 'hands-on' chief: he would often stop at a junior's drawing-board and plonk down an old-fashioned brass weight, of the sort once common in grocers' shops, of perhaps 16oz, and say to the young assistant, 'I want that weight saved from the rear suspension' – or whatever the man was responsible for. I (Brian Johnson) had the good fortune to meet Sir Alec (as he by then was) in the 1970s when he had formally retired but still had a consultant role and office at Longbridge. I was with James Burke and we were shooting a *Tomorrow's World* interview with Sir Alec on the likely form of the family car in 2000 (which then seemed a long way off). Sir Alec, then as always, talked with a felt pen in his hand. He drew, with incredible speed, accurate outlines of his ideas. He had always worked like that; professional draughtsmen who made the final detailed drawings have commented on the accuracy of Issigonis's freehand drawings. Incidentally, in that interview, Sir Alec correctly predicted that the petrol-engined small car would still be the norm in 2000, despite showing us his prototype steam-powered Mini, appropriately painted, as Sir Alec pointed out, fire-engine red!

In September 1956, before a firm decision about the 1100 had been made, the Suez crisis intervened. The consequent fuel shortages and a return to petrol rationing allowed the abstemious and continental bubble cars to begin to gain a serious toe-hold in the British market. These very small cars, the successors to the ephemeral 'cyclecars' of the early 1920s, were powered by small motor-cycle air-cooled engines and had just two seats. Two of the most popular ones were both German: the Heinkel and the Messerschmitt. The main, indeed some would say the only, virtue of the cars was a phenomenal fuel economy, and they were made very popular by the reintroduction of petrol rationing caused by the Suez crisis. In March 1957, therefore, Leonard Lord briefed Issigonis, as a matter of urgency, to design a small BMC car that would drive the bubble cars off British roads for good. Issigonis achieved this with a design coded ADO 15 (Austin Drawing Office 15), which became rather better known as the Mini.

Although the 1957 ADO 15 project was to be the brainchild and the last car wholly designed by Issigonis, he still had other responsibilities: the BMC 1100 and the 1800, both of which Issigonis was concerned with, though they would enter production guided by others. The Minor, on the other hand, remained very much the personal responsibility of Issigonis. In 1957 these cars still had fourteen years of production ahead of them and the popular Traveller had been successfully introduced. The 948cc Austin A-series engine had just been fitted to all saloons, which were now badged as the BMC Minor 1000, with the divided windscreen at last replaced by the curved one-piece screen it should have had in the first place.

Among many detail changes had been the fitting, in October 1956, of a glove-box lid with both the lid and the small knob designed by Issigonis – the Minor being still very much 'his' car. He must have been gratified at its success; for in those relatively affluent times, the 'never had it so good' years as Prime Minister Harold Macmillan

put it, some middle-class families could and did afford a second car. The Minor was, by some margin, the most popular choice. Although it was not bought by women in significant numbers, it was driven by women to a very large extent in those days before the advent of more equal status for women when the lives of most middle-class 'housewives' were prescribed by domesticity. A trip to the shops before the arrival of the superstores would reveal Minors parked in the high streets all over the UK, or engaged on the daily school run, or picking up their husbands from the railway stations. Women loved the Minors. These small cars were what today would be termed 'user-friendly'; they had an endearing quality absent from the competing perpendicular Ford Anglia or the Austin A30 – which, despite having the same A-series engine as the Minor, was slower, because of the better body shape that Issigonis had designed for the Minor.

The appeal of the Minor series was not, however, unique to women. Young male drivers who fancied themselves as Fangio, Mike Hawthorn or Stirling Moss could indulge their fantasy with road-holding which flattered their driving. In addition, as mentioned above, the Minors were not intimidating; their performance was good but containable. As one owner observed of her Minor: 'It never ran away with me.' The early long, whippy gear shift selecting the syncromesh gears did what it was supposed

It has long been the unshakable belief among the press offices of British motor manufacturers that young women with as little clothing on as possible sell cars – overlooking the undeniable fact that most men, who form the bulk of the car-buying public, will be looking at the women and not the car. This picture is an early case: one of the first batch of production 'Morris Mini Minors' as the original caption puts it (thereby coining a new word in English), enlivened by two rather incongruously bathing-costume-clad young ladies who were, it seems, so eager to get to the photo-call they had omitted to register their new 'Mini Minor'.

The cover of the 1959 Morris Mini Minor catalogue. 'Wizardry on Wheels' it proclaims as the Mini is launched. It cost just £496 tax paid – a figure which was too low to make any realistic profit. (Ford engineers who costed a 1959 Mini calculated that each car would lose the makers £10.) The artwork depicts the new car accurately enough but the artist has taken some licence with the spacing of driver and passenger and placed the children in the back to make the saloon seem roomy.

to do and the hydraulic brakes were as good as any other contemporary car. Minors were also seen by families as 'friendly' cars, and often had pet names given to them. Most Minors had lost sweets jammed down the back of the seats, which were often covered with dog hairs, and many Minors always seemed to have a pair of shoes on the back floor or wellies in the boot, invariably accompanied by an old coat. Under the carpets there was perhaps a layer of sand from a day-trip to the seaside. The narrow shelf in front of the driver contained, as likely as not, an AA book, maps, shopping lists, I-spy games, sweets, a dog-eared driver's handbook, a box of tissues, a duster and a torch (with flat battery). Minor saloons were remembered nostalgically long after the car had been replaced by a more modern and coldly efficient usurper, which no one cared much about.

The Minor continued to sell well, the peak year being 1958 when 115,000 were sold, and the Minor was the first British-built car to sell a million units. This milestone was reached on 22 December 1960, when the millionth Minor, a saloon, left the Longbridge production lines. During the celebrations Lord Nuffield was sufficiently moved to speak directly to Alec Issigonis for the first and only known time, gruffly thanking him for the Minor's success. The occasion was also marked by the release of 350 Minor 'Millions' painted in lilac with white upholstery and commemorative '1,000,000' badges. Normal production continued. In 1962 the final engine was fitted. This was a new BMC power unit of 1098cc, though the cars were still badged as 1100s. With the demise of BMC, production of Minor saloons was ended by their successors, British Leyland, in November 1970. The last Minors to be built were light commercial vehicles and Travellers which, in 1971, ended a 23-year production run of no fewer than 1,619,857 units of which 1,293,331 were saloons, Travellers or the very rare open convertibles. The remainder were commercial vans and pick-ups.

Early in its production, BMC had tried to coin the slogan 'the people's car' – perhaps overlooking the fact that the Germans had beaten them to it before the war with Volkswagen, which means, literally, 'people's car'. But what's in a name? The Minor was the first classless car and was driven by at least one Archbishop of Canterbury, a lord or two, some Grand Prix drivers who knew good handling when they saw it, and a million or so 'ordinary' and satisfied owners. Around 150,000 Minors survive worldwide. There are about 65,000 known to exist at the time of writing (1999) in the UK. They are for the most part highly prized by their owners. Minors are not difficult to keep roadworthy and MOT legal as there are dedicated clubs and dealers eager to supply all spare parts from a new engine, body parts, all the forty-two ash mouldings for the Traveller and even that knob on the glove-box lid. (Dropped on the driver's side, incidentally, in 1961, but restored for the passenger in 1964.) Minors, particularly the later 1098cc-engined 1100 cars, can safely be driven in modern traffic, though no Minor was produced with disc brakes (the hydraulic drum brakes are good examples of the type). Only a very few late Minors, and police panda cars, had an alternator as original equipment, the standard unit being the far less efficient dynamo, though many have since been converted to alternator electrics. However, compared with today's electronically dependent cars, the Minors have a very simple and undemanding 12-volt electrical system whose low amperage needs are well catered for by a modern 'maintenance-free' battery and dynamo. The road-holding and light, precise steering of all Minors are as good as any modern car in an urban environment, and a well-maintained Minor will give around 38mpg. Any good Minor is worth having but the most desirable – and expensive – from the collector's point of view, is the rare convertible (a rag-top in the USA). Only 3,600 were produced in a six-year run (1963–9). Incidentally, if one is offered a Minor convertible the watchword is *caveat emptor* as unscrupulous sellers have been known to hack off the top of a saloon, fit a hood and pretend it is a genuine convertible.

Sadly, neither Morris Motors, the Nuffield Organization nor British Leyland made much money from the Minor, despite the million-plus sales and the long production run of the car. It is thought that the maximum profit never exceeded £10 per unit, and often less. Although popular at home, it was less so when exported; this was partly because of the lack of overseas market research, resulting in cars with no heaters being sent to Finland and cars without special air cleaners and enlarged radiators going to Australia. The Volkswagen Beetle, in many ways an inferior design, outsold the Minor during the production years in the ratio of 15:1. (The number of VWs sold to date (1999) is an all-time record at over 21 million; it overtook the Ford Model T's 15 million sales in 1972.) In the lucrative US market the Minor, on the back of the outstanding sales of the TC MGs, should have made a killing but it failed to do so. Why? The answer is service. Volkswagen had a coast-to-coast network of dedicated dealers while the Minor had none. Spare parts were slow in arriving and the general sales backup was perceived, possibly unfairly, as poor and indifferent. The cars sold to overseas markets, even the late 1100s, were considered to be underpowered but the makers paid little or no attention. The Minors were also insufficiently advertised abroad, particularly in the USA. That said, today Minors all over the world, including the USA, are now highly prized possessions. Unlike the Volkswagen Beetle, which is still in production in Mexico, the Minor, despite stories to the contrary, is not. If you covet one, you will have to look in the classified ads. A final word: the asking price for a fully professionally restored Minor is around £7,000. If, however, you must have the very best, the Bath Minor Centre sold a late 1100 Traveller restored to *concours* condition for £15,000 in 1998. This would have amused 'that foreign chap' who started it all fifty years ago!

It is always fascinating to speculate as to what might have been. If Alec Issigonis, for example, had been able to complete his work on the V8 Alvis in 1952 would he have designed what is unquestionably one of the great cars of all time, the Mini? It is possible that Leonard Lord, who had a high regard for Issigonis's talents, would still have been able to lure him back from the up-market Alvis, to the small-car fold. Small cars were almost an obsession with Issigonis. The Minor had been a major step to liberate the family car from the pre-war image of a minimal vehicle built down to the lowest possible price. The Ford Anglia produced from 1939 to 1968, and therefore in direct competition with the Morris Minor, had no significant technical advances over the earlier Model Y designed in 1933. It was the appearance of the Morris Minor, which, despite a retrograde side-valve engine, took the 10hp family-car market by storm and sent designers scurrying to their drawing-boards. For Issigonis, the Minor was a justification of his ambition. If the Lightweight Special is discounted, the Minor was the first car he had designed more or less single-handed; it was his concept. As mentioned, Issigonis was to admit that he wanted to build the Minor with a transverse engine and front-wheel drive but he 'did not then know how to do it'. It is a measure of his ability that he did not, as many would have done, simply copy another design, the Citroën *Traction Avant*, for example, which had been in production from 1934. For Issigonis, the front-wheel drive for the Minor had to be his, or at least a system that he fully understood and could adapt and develop. The Minor of 1948 was therefore the art of the possible; it was innovative but constrained – in the case of the front-wheel drive by Issigonis himself, in the rejection of the flat-four engine by politics and by costing. In reality, if the Issigonis engine had been fitted, it is probable that the Minor would have been less successful than it in fact was. An unconventional and untried engine was bound to have had shortcomings that would have been apparent only when the engine was in production since, even with a dated Morris engine (which cannot have been expensive to produce), the cars made little enough money. With a new engine, making possible heavy claims under warranty, they may well have made even less or none. In that case the Minor, instead of becoming a classic, would have been just a lost cause.

THE CREATION OF THE MINI

It is not too fanciful to consider the Minor as a staging post to the Mini, which was as large an increment over the Minor as the Minor had been over the pre-war Morris Eight. That said, it is doubtful if Issigonis could have gone straight to the Mini in 1948, and even had he been able to do so, it is most unlikely that the Nuffield board – to say nothing of Lord Nuffield himself – would have sanctioned such a radical step from a man Lord Nuffield did not like and who had yet to prove he could design his

A typical Alec Issigonis freehand sketch, done no doubt as he was explaining the details to a colleague. The drawings, though done at speed, were surprisingly accurate. Interestingly, in this early Mini proposal, the petrol tank is shown in the engine compartment; on production Minis it was in the boot.

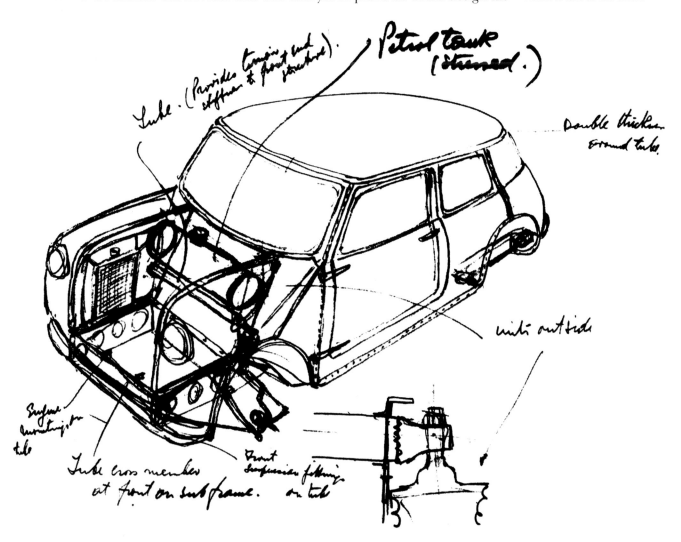

The original 1959 Mini engine with the gearbox and final drive train contained within what would be the sump of a conventional power unit. Issigonis, in grafting a standard production engine to his brilliant compact and space-saving concept, caused misgiving in less imaginative engineers: the hot engine oil would, they maintained, be too thin for the highly loaded transmission gears. In the event, apart from some difficulty during development with clutch slip, the units worked reliably, not only on the road cars but also with the highly stressed competition Cooper S Minis.

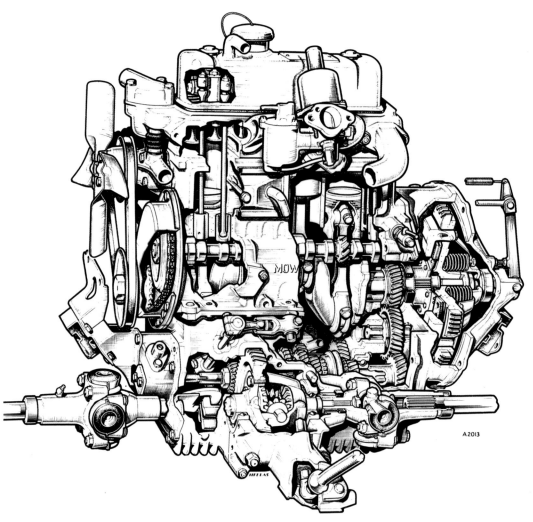

first car. Indeed, it is possible that if the Mini had appeared in 1948, the car-buying public would not have been ready for it. The Minor prepared the way by being just sufficiently advanced to give owners a glimpse of the advantages of future technological design trends.

When Issigonis received the remit from Leonard Lord to 'sweep the bubble cars off the British roads for good', he at once raised the question (no doubt with the engine difficulties that had beset and delayed the Minor in mind) of the powerplant envisaged for the ADO 15 project. 'You can have any engine you like, provided it is in current BMC production . . .' said Lord. This was both good news and bad news. The only possible engine to fall within Lord's stricture was the current Austin 948cc ohv A-series unit. With that as the foundation, Issigonis and his hand-picked team set to work with clean sheets of paper on their drawing-boards to fulfil the ADO 15 requirement. The outcome, the Mini, is still – in 1999 – in production at Rover, very largely as Sir Alec Issigonis, who died in 1988, designed it. The Mini cannot therefore strictly be considered yet as a classic car – though it is definitely a classic in waiting. Moreover, such was the influence of this car during the 1960s, and beyond, that many consider the Mini not only a potential classic but one of the great cars of all time, alongside the Model T Ford and the Volkswagen Beetle – and not even those cars coined a new word for the English language. We will therefore describe the beginnings of ADO 15, a.k.a. the Morris 'Mini' Minor as it was originally known. (There was also a short-lived 'Austin Seven'-badged Mini but it was soon to disappear.)

The Mini, like the Minor, was an Issigonis design from front bumper to rear. Practically every detail of the car was innovative and radical. Each and every facet was sketched out by Issigonis with a felt pen while he was in conference with his colleagues. By July 1957, in the remarkably short time of four months, a full-size wooden mock-up was made, revealing for the first time the now familiar shape, right down to the external body welds. The body shape was nearly finalized and the running gear was to be the next consideration.

The early decision to have front-wheel drive was not original. The pre-war Czech Tracta, French Hotchkiss and the well-known Citroën Light 15 all had front-wheel drive, but front-wheel drive with a transverse-mounted engine had not been seen since the Christie, a long-forgotten Gorden Bennett racing car of 1903 – and that monster had direct drive to the wheels. Issigonis's reasoning to use a transverse engine was simple. An in-line four-cylinder engine is roughly three times longer than it is wide; if you place the engine sideways you are allowing for a useful increase in the volume of the passenger space. Assuming a 6ft 8in wheelbase, Issigonis sketched out a box 10 x 4 x 4ft, which allowed 1ft 6in for the boot and 6ft 6in for the driver and the three passengers, with the remaining 2ft being sufficient to accommodate the transverse engine and clutch. Mounted conventionally (that is, north/south) the A-series engine – the unit of choice – measured 3ft 2in; if it was mounted transversely the width would be just 18in.

Although the transverse option seemed an elegant solution, there was a difficulty – the positioning of the gearbox and clutch within the restricted space between the front-wheel arches. The solution Issigonis arrived at was bold; he proposed combining the transmission gears and differential within the sump of the A-series engine. This was a shock! Gears needed special lubricants, not hot, thin, dirty engine oil. Issigonis took the view that oil was oil and that there would be no problem; events were to prove him correct. The engine, though transversely mounted, had been chosen with Leonard Lord's dictum in mind; it was a standard BMC 948cc ohv A-series production unit. At least, most of it was from the crankshaft upwards; below the crankshaft a new alloy casting replaced the standard tin sump and contained not only the engine oil but also the contents of the four-speed and reverse gearbox, the differential and the drive shafts to the front wheels. The more-or-less standard clutch was rigged outboard of the crankcase, returning the drive to the primary gear and input shaft of the four gears. The entire unit was compact and fitted easily within the restricted 2ft engine space.

On the early prototype car the engine was mounted west/east, that is with the inlet manifold facing the front of the car, and the radiator was mounted to the right, with a fan drawing air from the offside wheel arch. During testing – which revealed to the astonished test drivers a maximum speed of 96mph – it was discovered that the carburettor was tending to ice up in damp weather so a decision was made to reverse the engine to an east/west configuration, with air warmed by the exhaust keeping carburettor ice at bay. The problem then was that the drive direction was also reversed; the gearbox offering four reverse gears and only one forward! It would have been possible to redesign the camshaft to enable the engine to run clockwise, but not only the camshaft was involved; if the direction of rotation was reversed, the oil, water pumps and starter, and several thrust bearings, would also have to be changed and the resultant engine would hardly fulfil Leonard Lord's insistence about using current production engines. Issigonis had already stretched that restriction to the limit. The rotation question was solved by the positioning of an idler gear, which restored the drive to an anti-clockwise direction. At the same time the capacity of the engine was slightly reduced to 848cc by shortening the stroke of the pistons.

The Mini Estate was not as popular as the Minor Traveller had been, perhaps because it was too small. However, the original Mini Estate sold over 200,000 units. Unlike the Minor Traveller, the woodwork of the Estate was purely decorative and had no structural significance; it was also expensive to produce.

Issigonis had a walk around the prototype and decided that the width had to be increased by 2in (the bumpers had already been ordered)! During the testing with the revised engine position, it was discovered that there existed an area of low pressure inside the wheel arches; this was utilized by making the fan blow air through the radiator core into the low pressure, with the astonishing result that the size of the radiator could safely be reduced by some 20 per cent.

The most difficult problem facing the Issigonis team was the design of the front-wheel drive. The basic difficulty was simply the unfortunate fact that the front wheels, in addition to rotating, had to be capable of turning to steer the car. Early attempts at front-wheel drive failed because designers, among them the great Ettore Bugatti, had not realized that the usual universal joint, of the type found on the propeller shafts of most cars and lorries, cannot be used to drive steerable wheels because it is not a 'constant-velocity' coupling. It is certain that Alec Issigonis knew of the problems associated with front-wheel drive and he had, from the first, decided to use a constant-velocity joint patented by a Czech engineer named Rzeppa. This coupling had originally been developed before the war by an English engineer, William Cull,

Sir Alec Issigonis on the occasion, in 1969, of the 1,000,000th Mini leaving the production lines – it is doubtful if any present that day, including Sir Alec himself, would have believed that a further 4,364,074 Minis would have followed by 1999, when 350 Minis a week were still being produced and probably will continue to be so into the twenty-first century.

Glory days. The Hopkirk/Liddon Cooper S Mini competing in the 1964 Monte Carlo rally which, to the consternation of the French, it won.

who had also designed the famous Scott motor cycles. The Rzeppa joint, in essentials, is a special form of caged, captive ball race with the outer track slotted, allowing it to be turned up to 40 degrees while maintaining the driven input and output shafts at a constant velocity. The Rzeppa joints for the Mini were made to Issigonis's specification by a British specialist firm – Birfield – and they performed exactly as required. The drive shafts of the Mini required two universal joints each side, the steerable outer joint and an inner joint which took the drive from the differential, this being a simple Hook or Carden universal joint that accommodated the up-and-down movements of the suspension. Since the angles were restricted to a maximum of around 14 degrees, and the inner drive shafts did not turn with the wheels, the more expensive constant-velocity couplings were not necessary. The production Minis used an inner universal joint that had rubber elements specially designed by Alex Moulton. Issigonis had designed the Mini to have fully independent suspension on all four wheels. The rear wheels were mounted on trailing arms which had ball-race bearings with steel balls and a nylon race. The 'springing' of all the wheels was by Moulton-designed units, which used rubber cones in compression (perhaps a reminder of the

Lightweight). All the early cars and the competition Minis had the simple rubber cones, and later Minis had the BMC 1100/1300 'Hydrolastic' fluid system augmenting the rubber in compression. This system did make the ride more even, but competition drivers preferred the early non-connected system.

Even the Mini's road wheels were non-standard – they were an unheard-of size of 10in. At that time only wheelbarrows and scooters had such small wheels. Experts at Dunlop agreed to supply the required tyres. Then followed 30,000 miles of testing, mostly at night on the BMC testing routes around Oxfordshire or on the perimeter track of a disused RAF airfield at Chalgrove (Chalgrove was not quite disused; Martin-Baker used it for the first 'live' ejection tests of their now-famous seats). In July 1958, just fifteen months after he had briefed Issigonis to design the ADO 15 car, the prototype Mini, called the 'Orange Box' by the test drivers (that was the colour), was presented to Leonard Lord for a test drive. Alec Issigonis accompanied him as he drove the first Mini around the works roads at Longbridge. After about five minutes he stopped the car, turned to Issigonis and said, 'Alec, this is it, I want it in production within twelve months.' Issigonis simply replied: 'Sir Leonard, this will cost millions of

Paddy Hopkirk with 33 EJB, the winning car, with some silver. The scene is Monte Carlo just after the prizegiving for the 1964 event. A Mini also won the 1965 event and although Paddy Hopkirk finished first in the 1966 rally his Mini was denied a hat-trick as the French disqualified the car on the flimsy grounds that the headlight dipping did not comply with the regulations. A French Citroën was declared the winner. In the end, the world's sporting press gave BMC much more publicity for not winning than would have been the case if the true result had been allowed to stand.

The greatest invention
since the wheel.

pounds.' 'Don't worry about that, I shall sign the cheques, you get on with getting the thing to work.' Thus, without board meetings, stylists, costings by an army of accountants or even any significant market research, a very great car went into production. Up to that moment, it had cost BMC an estimated £100,000 for the prototypes and experimental work, all of which had been performed by a team that could be counted on the fingers of two hands. It could not happen that way now.

The Mini consolidated what the Minor had started. It is a totally classless gender-free car that appeals to both men and women, young and old alike. The virtues of the Mini remain many and various whether competing in – and winning – international rallies and road races, taking the children to school or shopping at supermarkets. Its appeal is universal and even when, some time in the twenty-first century, the last Mini leaves the production lines its influence, and that of Sir Alec Issigonis, will continue in the new generation of family cars into the foreseeable future.

Opposite **A 1970 BMC poster which says it all. The Mini clubman, loathed by some purists, does not differ much from the Sir Alec's original concept.**

CHAPTER TWO

THE FASHIONS OF THE 1960S

*I*N EUROPE, almost to the end of the 1950s, the mere possession of a car was a status symbol in itself. The number of cars had been edging up, but slowly. In the UK, for example, there had been 2 million cars registered as being in use in 1939, just before the outbreak of the Second World War. During the war, of course, no new cars were being built to replace those that died through old age or enemy action, and it was 1949 before the 1939 total was exceeded. By the end of 1959 the number had just edged through the 5 million mark. In practice, this meant that around 1 British household in 6 had a car. Even this was enough to be making a nonsense of the planning considerations for the early new towns, for example, in which parking and garage provision had been based on a car ownership rate of 1 per 10 households. Ten years later, however, the number of cars in use in the UK had more than doubled, to 11.5 million. One effect of this increase was that it was no longer enough to boast 'we have a car'; you had to be able to boast about what kind of car you had.

In the UK, before the war, a kind of social hierarchy had grown up around the old RAC horsepower rating scale, an obscure calculation that had almost nothing to do with real horsepower but was used as the charging basis for the road fund licence. A 'Seven' was the most basic family runabout; the 'Eight' was the staple transport of middle-class families; the 'Ten' was for the bank manager and the headmaster; and the 'Twelve' was for the doctor and the solicitor. Anything rated higher than this was for the distinctly rich, while at the other end of the scale, the 'Seven' – in the form of the Austin Seven – may have been dreamed up as a car for the masses, but you have to remember that of those 2 million cars in 1939 there was only 1 for every 25 people. There had to be many more vehicles on the road before the car became a consumer durable, and a highly visible one. That in turn meant that looks – and reputations – became very important.

Car advertising in the 1960s threw up some strange scenarios in the interests of creating an 'ideal' motoring world and making cars attractive. One can only wonder why this young man has turned his back on the two young ladies in the Triumph Vitesse convertible (the Vitesse was a six-cylinder conversion of the Herald) in order to make for a saloon version of the same car ...

This was already a familiar situation for the Americans. By the end of 1959 there were almost 60 million cars in use in the USA. If you threw in trucks and buses, that meant there was a vehicle of some kind for every 2 people – compared with 1 for every 8 people in the UK and France, 1 for every 11 people in West Germany, and 1 for every 23 people in Italy. By the end of the decade, those figures had become 1 vehicle per 4.2 people in the UK, 1 per 3.5 people in France, 1 per 4.4 people in West Germany and 1 per 5.3 people in Italy. In other words, even if Europe had not quite, in 1969, reached the American level of 1959, it was well on the way.

In Europe, however, the results of market growth throughout the 1960s were very different. In the USA, intense competition in a huge free market had seen the smaller and less efficient manufacturers driven out of business, even if they made attractive products. In the end, there were only three giant companies that really mattered: Chrysler, Ford and General Motors. This 'big three' competed with each other to some extent on the basis of power, price and appearance, but mainly on power and appearance. What Americans did not do was to indulge in genuine technical innovation. It was the Europeans who, during the 1960s, seriously embraced front-wheel drive, overhead camshaft engines, radial-ply tyres, halogen headlamps and independent rear suspensions, to take only the most obvious examples. But where price was concerned, the American 'big three' were producing enough cars to be well along the economy-of-scale curve; they tracked each other's 'base' model prices ferociously, with cars that made them little if any money. Their profits came from the higher-range models to which skilled and enthusiastic salesmen directed buyers' attention. Why have this under-powered version with its manual gearbox and basic equipment when for a few hundred dollars more you could have a V8 engine, automatic transmission, radio, record player and air conditioning?

Where styling was concerned, the important thing in the USA was to buy the styling features that meant the neighbours would know you were driving this year's car: the ornate grille, the double headlamps, the bigger tailfins. There had always been an interest in design in the USA, and the 1950s had seen designers there define the 'post-war look', a kind of revolution in which body shapes became 'blended', with front grilles horizontal rather than vertical, and in which running-boards vanished. (Today's youngsters might ask what running-boards were, but, without them, cars wouldn't have been able to charge through Al Capone's Chicago with gun-toting gangsters or special agents clinging to both sides.)

By the 1960s, designers were wondering where to go next. The answer was not obvious, especially once it became clear that design was such a crucial sales factor, and during the late 1950s and into the 1960s some of its aspects became extremely dubious. Styling was changed not so much to make cars look better, but rather to make them visibly different from last year's models. American cars simply became bigger and bigger, and more and more ostentatious.

Above **For those who recognize it, the southern corner of Trafalgar Square, some time in the mid-1960s (note the Austin 1100 and the Ford Cortina Estate). But apart from the scooter rider, observe also two Humber Super Snipes in simultaneous view, one at centre left and the other emerging from the front of the bus. Given the proximity of Whitehall, one imagines that one or both were on official business.**

Left **A coast-bound bank holiday traffic jam on the A20 towards the end of the 1960s. Apart from indicating that the motor car was by then well established as a cause of congestion, this picture shows that the imported car had yet to make much of an impact on the British motoring scene. Of the clearly identifiable cars in this stream, only three are foreign: one Renault 16 and two Volkswagen Beetles. Ten years later, the picture would have been very different.**

At its best, American design from the drawing-boards of men like Raymond Loewy, Harley Earle, Virgil Exner and Bill Mitchell could be superb, especially when they went back to first principles to create a completely new model. Even today, experts still admire the General Motors design chief Bill Mitchell's first Buick Riviera. It was the way these designs were 'developed' from one model year to the next, with non-functional features added and then exaggerated, which offended most Europeans – and, to be fair, a lot of sensitive and educated Americans who recognized built-in obsolescence when they saw it. Yet the American sales figures proved the point: styling sold cars. The European manufacturers, seeing their own market growing at last and knowing they would have to fight for their share of it, began to take design more seriously.

A DIFFERENT WAY OF DOING THINGS

Europe and the UK could not go the American way. Their cars could not be allowed to grow, from one year to the next, into anything like the Chevrolet Impala, the Ford Fairlane or the Chrysler New Yorker. European towns and roads were not built for cars that size, and most European governments taxed any car of more than modest proportions in a way that discouraged their purchase by any but the rich. Worse still, European petrol was already taxed at levels that Americans would have found difficult to understand. Fuel economy didn't really matter to the American buyer, but it certainly did to the British, the French and the Germans – and even more to the Italians.

Because they could not make their cars big and bold, almost to the point of brash and defiant ugliness in the American fashion, the Europeans sought genuine beauty. They didn't always find it, but they scored many successes. Many of the best designs of the decade came from Italy, from the studios of masters like Pininfarina, Bertone, Ghia and Vignale. They sought their beauty in purity of shape, a balance of mass, and clever but restrained detailing. They paraded their most advanced ideas at the major motor shows, most of all at Geneva, in Paris, and on their home ground in Turin, and the world's motor industry came to look at their design studies. The Americans, for the most part, shook their heads and said it was all too sophisticated for the average American buyer – which may have been a slur on those buyers, especially in view of the growing success of imports in the US market. The rest of the world generally admired what they saw, and the Italian design houses began to sign consultancy contracts with other European companies, and with the Japanese.

Compared with the American example, the other thing that did not happen in Europe was any great rationalization of the industry into a small number of very powerful groups. The reason was simple enough. The USA was a single country. In Europe, there were four potentially powerful vehicle-producing countries (the UK, France, West Germany and Italy) to which a determined and capable Sweden probably needed to be added. Each of these countries supported a number of manufacturers, quite apart from the European operations of Ford and General Motors

Opposite *'Export or die' was the post-war watchword. British car manufacturers had to export two-thirds of their production; otherwise the government cut off their supplies of sheet steel. Thus cars like these very early Morris Minors and Morris Oxfords, awaiting loading on the quayside, were thrust into export markets for which they had never been developed, and whose motoring conditions they could not withstand.*

(Vauxhall in the UK, Opel in West Germany). Before there could be any kind of rationalization on a European scale, each country had to sort out its own industry, and that didn't happen during the 1960s. Indeed, it has barely happened by the end of the century. So Europe remained a patchwork quilt of car manufacturing, made up of companies with very different traditions, and some of them government-owned, like Renault in France and Alfa Romeo in Italy. What it meant was that no very powerful group could emerge to work on an American scale.

When the 1960s began, these European manufacturers were producing a motley collection of cars, reflecting each country's post-war situation and its philosophy. The UK hastened to convert its pre-war car factories from aircraft manufacture (which is what most of them had been doing) to car production. The Attlee government adopted a policy of 'export or die', making it difficult and expensive to build and sell cars in the home market and more or less forcing their car manufacturers to design and build for export. The French and the Italians on the other hand decided to 'get the country back on wheels', no matter how odd, ugly and underpowered the cars were, an attitude that gave the French the Citroën 2CV and the Renault 4CV. The French in particular made it difficult and expensive to build and sell big cars, and more or less forced their car manufacturers to build small, cheap, low-powered, eco-

During the 1960s, it became a minor sport to see how many people – preferably small, slim and agile young ladies – could cram themselves into a Mini. The rules usually stipulated that the car could still be driven, if only for a short distance and in a straight line. Some contests insisted that the occupants were fully contained; others, as here, allowed legs to emerge from windows. According to circumstances, the maximum recorded number is somewhere between the teens and the twenties.

nomical models which sold in their home market but were almost unexportable. The Italians were rather like the French, except that Alfa Romeo and Lancia went on building 'real' cars. As for the West Germans, they had first to reconstruct their industry from its shattered remains, with the help of the occupying powers (until it was rescued by reunification, East Germany was condemned by socialist planning to building small numbers of crude cars with two-stroke engines). As West Germany recovered, it built growing numbers of small and medium-sized cars for home consumption, not only the Volkswagen Beetle but also the Opel Kadett, and various Auto-Unions and NSUs. But at the same time Mercedes built big cars as taxis and for export and were joined, as the 1960s progressed, by BMW.

For the British, 'export or die' proved a disaster. It would have been all right if the British cars built in the 1950s had been well engineered for export markets, but on the whole they were not. The British simply did not understand the real motoring needs of the USA, the biggest and juiciest export market of all, or even of its own Commonwealth countries. British manufacturers exported cars with a great fanfare, saw them come to grief, and failed either to learn the lessons or to provide the proper technical support. Before the end of the 1950s they had begun to realize the obvious and, with government restrictions finally removed, went instead for their home market and for Europe. That was a much more successful approach which, as we have already seen in Chapter One, gave rise at the end of the 1950s to Alec Issigonis's masterpiece, the Mini.

MINI IMPACT

With hindsight, it is easy to see the Mini as one of the crucial designs in motoring history, its transverse-engine, front-drive layout quickly copied in Europe and, after a longer interval, becoming the standard (for all but the largest and heaviest cars) throughout the world. At the time, its impact was less obvious. For at least a year after its introduction, people thought it a distinctly odd little beast, and distrusted its apparent mechanical complexity. It was only when they began to realize the claims were true – that it was roomy enough for four despite its tiny size, extremely economical, and capable of going round corners amazingly fast – that they warmed to it. Certainly the Mini was helped by its 'cheeky' looks, astonishingly achieved by Alec Issigonis and a handful of engineering draughtsmen without a 'stylist' in sight. They were looks which seemed to appeal specially to women. The Mini quickly numbered a higher proportion of women among its buyers than any previous British car. As the 1960s became the decade in which a generation of young women flexed the muscles of their independence, it was the Mini more than anything that made them mobile. From time to time, photographers clustered around one of the little cars while teams of attractive (and slim) young women competed to see just how many of them could get into it at the same time while still allowing it to be driven. The record is reputed to have been somewhere in the mid-teens . . .

Apart from its contribution to female emancipation, the Mini also became class-less. People who would not normally be seen dead in a 'nasty, cheap little car' arrived at special events in the full glare of publicity, in Alec Issigonis's masterpiece. Many of them ordered specially trimmed and equipped versions from a number of specialist converters, of whom Radford, and Wood and Pickett, were two of the best known and most successful. They realized that there was money to be made here just when the traditional coachwork trade was on its last legs. Customers like Peter Sellers instituted a kind of competition to see how expensive you could justifiably make a Mini; nobody was afraid to be seen in one.

BMC failed to predict the way things would go. The Mini was going to be 'badge-engineered' like all its other models. It was actually launched as the Austin Seven and the Morris Mini-Minor but to its public it immediately became 'the Mini'. Nevertheless, for a long time afterwards if you looked carefully you would see that Minis carried either Austin or Morris badges. Nobody but the BMC sales force really cared.

The Mini became one of the principal symbols of the emerging 'classless society' and many celebrities bought the car for modification to luxury standard by coachbuilding companies. Here, Peter Sellers emerges at speed from Britt Ekland's 'birthday cake' in her present, a Mini given the luxury treatment by Harold Radford, one of the most prominent companies in this specialist business. Money was the only thing which determined how much walnut, leather and gadgetry went inside.

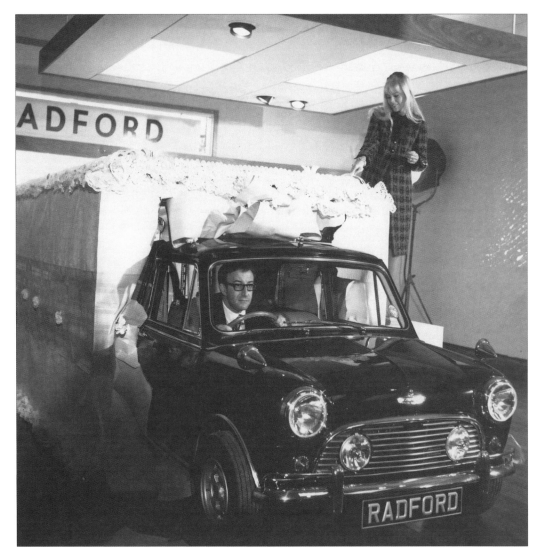

NON-MINI OPTIONS

In 1960, it must be remembered, there were still five companies building family cars on a large scale in Britain, and three of them – BMC, Rootes and Standard-Triumph – were British-owned, the other two being Ford and Vauxhall. To these you could add the more specialized cars coming from Rover and Jaguar, both still independent, plus Rolls-Royce and a number of comparative 'tiddlers', including Lotus, Jensen, Morgan and Reliant, as well as others who tended to come and go. Already gone was Jowett, forced out of business by its rivals – some suggest – because its adventurous engineering was winning it too many friends, even if others still remember having to remove the front wheels of the Jowett Javelin to change the sparking plugs in its flat-four engine.

In terms of actual names the British were even better off, since this was the age of badge engineering in which BMC offered a choice of Austin, Morris, MG, Riley, Wolseley and Vanden Plas models, while the Rootes Group weighed in with Hillman, Humber, Singer and Sunbeam. The essence of badge engineering was that you took a single basic car and dressed it up in a number of ways, with different radiator grilles and trim packages – and, of course, different badges – in an attempt to broaden its market. One should not be too rude about badge engineering, which had been – and still is – practised with great success, and rather more subtlety, by General Motors in the USA (Buick, Chevrolet, Oldsmobile, Pontiac).

BMC's special problem was that it relied on badge engineering in a market which wasn't big enough really to need it, and devoted too much energy in that direction when it should have been working on more fundamental issues. By 1960 it was producing three main car ranges apart from the Mini. These were a 'compact' car range embracing the Morris Minor, the Austin A40, the Wolseley 1500 and the Riley 1.5 (the latter two being, in effect, a rebodied Minor fitted with the 1.5-litre B-series engine replacing the 1-litre A-series); its stable family car range, soon to be restyled by Pininfarina and consisting of the Austin Cambridge, the Morris Oxford and their badge-engineered MG, Wolseley and Riley equivalents; and the big Austin Westminster, discussed in more detail in Chapter Four. BMC was also building its sports cars (see Chapter Three), the Austin-Healeys and MGs. The company's main game-plan for the 1960s was to develop a range of front-driven 'enlarged Minis' to replace all but the big cars and the sports cars. As we shall see, it was an idea that began well and then went disastrously wrong; so wrong that the successor to BMC, which in its day was truly huge, not only in the UK but with significant manufacturing operations in Belgium, Italy, Spain and Australia, would eventually have gone to the wall had it not been rescued by nationalization.

The family-owned Rootes Group, meanwhile, enjoyed a solid reputation for worthy, well-built, if rather heavy and uneconomical, medium-sized and larger cars, its big seller being the Hillman Minx, badge-engineered into the alternative Singer

Gazelle and Sunbeam Rapier, and tough enough to enjoy a degree of rallying success with drivers like Peter Harper until the Mini-Cooper became all-conquering. Its bigger cars, the Humber Hawk and Super Snipe (see Chapter Four), were equally well regarded even if they did not sell in large numbers. Rootes' plan for the 1960s unfortunately hinged around an attempt to win a share of the Mini market with a completely new and radically engineered car, the Imp. A little further down the line, it was foreseen that the Minx/Gazelle/Rapier range would be replaced by a new, lighter, roomier and more efficient (and hopefully more profitable) design. Unfortunately, the Imp was to prove an almost unmitigated disaster, while the Minx replacement was delayed until it was too late to do any good.

Standard-Triumph entered the 1960s with a new small car, the Herald, which might have been thought radical if the Mini had not upstaged it. The Herald was distinguished by an astonishingly small turning circle – at some cost in front-tyre wear, if

The Wolseley 1500 was really no more than a Morris Minor with a bigger engine – the 1.5-litre B-series replacing the 1-litre A-series – and a more upright, squared-off body. The once-famous hallmark of the Wolseley, the front grille badge illuminated at night by a small internal bulb, is clearly in evidence, as are the chromed wing mirrors which gave either a very limited or a very distorted field of view.

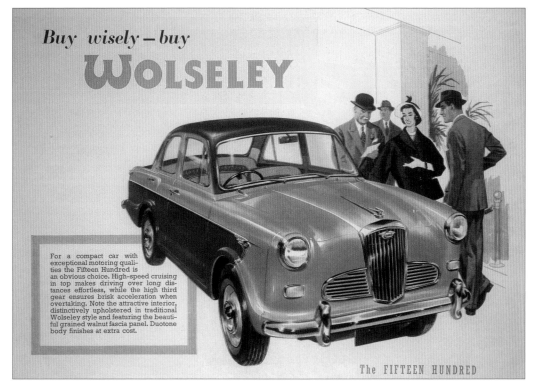

Buy wisely – buy

WOLSELEY

For a compact car with exceptional motoring qualities the Fifteen Hundred is an obvious choice. High-speed cruising in top makes driving over long distances effortless, while the high third gear ensures brisk acceleration when overtaking. Note the attractive interior, distinctively upholstered in traditional Wolseley style and featuring the beautiful grained walnut fascia panel. Duotone body finishes at extra cost.

The FIFTEEN HUNDRED

Left **Advertising promotion for cars like the Wolseley 1500 leaned heavily on its essential 'Britishness', as appreciated by the kind of people who wore hats. The effect is rather spoiled by the awful two-tone paint which was an American-inspired fashion of the 1960s. Note also that this car lacks the foglamps and wing mirrors of the 'real' car – and that its wipers are parked much more tidily!**

Below **The Triumph Herald may have been a bold attempt to create something different in the way of a small car, but equipping it with independent rear suspension without spending enough to do the job properly was a recipe for potential disaster. The Herald's swing-axle system could all too easily behave as shown – set up by co-author Daniels for a 1960s photographer. The speed is around 20mph . . .**

you used it very often – and by a swing-axle independent rear suspension which formed a considerable trap for the unwary. This did not stop Triumph making a more powerful version of the car (the Vitesse) or spinning off a couple of closely related sports cars, the Spitfire and the GT6 (see Chapter Three). Above the Herald, Triumph was close to launching a new medium-large car, the 2000, which, together with its rival the Rover 2000, was destined to revolutionize attitudes in the market towards 'executive' cars (see Chapter Four).

As for the British-based American companies, Ford was in reasonable shape. By 1960 it could offer the recently launched 105E Anglia with its reverse-raked rear window and its advanced (by the standards of the day) engine, supported by the 100E Popular, which was actually a cheap-and-cheerful version of the old-shape Anglia; the seemingly eternal medium-sized Consul; and the larger and more powerful Zephyr and Zodiac. What is more, Ford was on the verge of mounting a marketing master-stroke in the form of the original Cortina. Not everything it did would be touched by success, especially in the executive car class, but on the whole the 1960s would be a good decade for Ford.

The same could not be said for Vauxhall. In the 1950s the company had adopted a policy of making its cars

Above **The Vauxhall Viva was
the company's first attempt at
a small – but not too small –
car; in the 1960s, a Mini-sized
Vauxhall would have been
inconceivable to its American
masters at General Motors.
Entirely conventional, slab-
sided, efficient and easy to
drive, the Viva would certainly
have appealed to this
archetypal family in its then-
new 'town house'.**

Previous spread **The Hillman
Minx, in series after series, was
the staple product of the
Rootes Group, which was also
the proprietor of the Humber,
Singer and Sunbeam names.
Although needlessly heavy and
old-fashioned in some respects,
the four-seat, 1.6-litre Minx
was usually perceived as being
half a social class higher than
Austin or Morris, and certainly
one-up on Ford or Vauxhall.**

look like scaled-down American models. The first Victor, with its wrap-around wind-screen and huge chrome bumpers (through one corner of which the exhaust pipe emerged) was so bad that the normally obsequious road testers of *The Autocar* were driven to serious criticism of some of its aspects. Vauxhall withdrew its advertising from the magazine for six months but failed to take the hint: its bigger cars, the Velox and Cresta, were almost as bad. To make matters worse, its rust protection was so bad that its cars were becoming a standing joke. What was more, in 1960 Vauxhall had no small car to take on the Ford Anglia or Triumph Herald; it had plans for a not-quite-small one, which eventually emerged as the Viva.

MEANWHILE, IN EUROPE . . .

By 1960 the French motor industry had boiled itself down to four major companies: adventurous and idiosyncratic Citroën, then owned by the tyre company Michelin, a firm believer in front-wheel drive since 1934; solidly bourgeois Peugeot; state-owned Renault; and Chrysler-owned Simca. There was also the strange Panhard, a big streamlined car with a tiny two-cylinder engine, soon to vanish as a separate entity. Citroën, gloriously lacking in logic, made slow and utilitarian A-class cars – the 2CV and its spin-offs – and the big DS series, easily the most technically advanced car in the world, but nothing in between. It had plans to plug the gap, but nothing serious came of them (in the form of the GS) until 1970 by which time it was too late to prevent the company sliding into financial disaster and being sold to Peugeot.

Peugeot itself was plodding on with just two tough, honest, reliable cars, the medium-small 203 and the medium-large 403, and had plans to replace them both, the first with the radical 204 and the second with the Pininfarina-styled 404. Renault had recently introduced the pretty Dauphine, which won huge sales but then, through the early 1960s, revealed itself not only as a rust-bucket but also, being rear-engined and swing-axled, as suffering from potentially serious stability and handling problems. The company's bigger cars were on the slide, but it had adventurous, and eventually successful, plans to rescue itself with a switch to front-wheel drive. Simca was in the middle of taking an ill-judged decision to make an all-new small, rear-engined car to complement its range of stolid and not very appealing medium-sized models, the Aronde and, later, the 1300/1500. It would have been quite difficult, in 1960, to predict the much better shape in which the French industry found itself by 1970.

By 1959 Germany's motor industry had already pulled itself well out of its post-war disaster situation. Indeed, the writing was already on the wall for all to read: Germany's car production had overtaken that of the UK by 1956, and in 1959 the German industry made 1.5 million cars compared with the UK's 1.2 million. A great deal of this expansion was due to the success of Volkswagen, which made over 600,000 Beetles during the year, but there were substantial contributions from Opel, Ford, Mercedes and Auto-Union among others. Germany was also the prime source of bubble cars (see Chapter Five) but that market was in the process of bursting, and many of the companies involved – Goggomobil, Goliath, Lloyd – would disappear

The epitome of technical adventure in motoring in the 1960s was provided by the Citroën DS, seen here in production at the Quai de Javel factory in Paris (now bulldozed and replaced by a public park!). With its ingenious hydropneumatic suspension, serious attention to aerodynamics and other avant-garde features, the DS set standards which in some respects, especially of combined ride comfort and roadholding, have never been matched to this day.

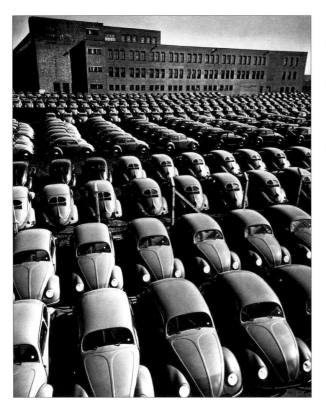

The Volkswagen factory at Wolfsburg, its reconstruction encouraged by the British Army of Occupation who bought much of its early output for use as staff cars, quickly built up production of the rear-engined Beetle, created before the war by Professor Porsche as Hitler's 'People's Car'. By the 1960s the Beetle was well on the way to becoming a legend, thanks largely to step-by-step development which, contrary to the American philosophy, left the car looking almost unchanged.

with it. BMW existed, but not on any scale: the 1960s would see it emerge as a real force, starting almost from scratch. Borgward was still in business, though not for much longer, and NSU was making small cars in modest numbers.

By 1960 Fiat was a growing giant, full of energy although not without its problems. It had long been committed to making a full range of cars, although its success in numbers was pinned to the small, rear-engined 500 and 600, which had done for Italy what the Citroën 2CV and Renault 4CV had done for France, if not quite to the same extent. But Fiat also offered the 1100, the 1400 and the 1900, and would soon add the neat little rear-engined 850. In the longer term, though, Fiat's fortunes were to be saved by a range of more modern products, including a switch to front-wheel drive for its best-sellers.

Fiat then had two Italian rivals, the privately owned Lancia and the state-owned Alfa Romeo. Years later it would end up owning them both, having bought Lancia (complete with all its debts) for a nominal lira, and later relieving the Italian government of the endless headache that Alfa Romeo had become. In 1960, however, Lancia was still well regarded, a maker of excellently engineered cars in the tradition of its founder, which through the 1960s would press ahead with its Fulvia and Flavia, even holding out the faint hope of a replacement for the big luxury Flaminia. As for Alfa Romeo, it was at the time the world's main proprietor of twin overhead camshaft engines for volume production cars, with its 1.3-litre Giulietta and 1.9-litre 1900.

. . . AND IN THE USA

The 1960s might have been relatively uneventful in the USA. The bare statistics almost suggest that they were. If you compare 1969 with 1959, you find that the American 'big three' made 8.2 million cars compared with 5 million, and those cars were mostly big and powerful, if not perhaps quite as chrome-laden and grotesque as those which had rolled off the Detroit production lines ten years earlier. Yet three things had happened to upset the smoothly-rolling scheme of things. More or less in the order in which they struck, they were safety, imports, and pollution.

Nobody, in designing American cars, had ever given serious thought to safety beyond avoiding the most obviously hazardous features. Many times a day on American roads, vehicles collided and people died; that was what happened in collisions. Then, suddenly, there appeared a book called *Unsafe at Any Speed*, written by a young lawyer called Ralph Nader. *Unsafe at Any Speed* took the American car industry apart.

To some extent he had been issued an invitation by General Motors, which had suffered one of its occasional strange, convulsive fits of advanced engineering and produced a six-cylinder, rear-engined car called the Chevrolet Corvair. The Corvair had swing-axle rear suspension rather like that of the Volkswagen Beetle, but with its much greater weight and power, it snapped a good deal more viciously if the driver became careless or over-ambitious. Nader started with the Corvair but then moved through many then-current American cars, pointing to feature after feature that had killed people in collisions simply because nobody had ever thought seriously about designing them so that they didn't. General Motors reacted to Nader's onslaught in the most self-destructive way: it hired detectives to dig some dirt out of his life. Not only did they not find any, but they also allowed Nader to discover what they were up to. From then on, the whole industry was pushed on to the defensive and, before long, the first legislation had appeared to force car makers to adopt minimum safety standards in designing their products. Things would never be quite the same again.

Then there were the imports. Because the USA had been a free market, as well as a huge one, ever since the end of the war, car makers elsewhere were eager to export to the USA if they thought they had a product that would sell. Nobody in the USA was very much worried if the Europeans could sell a few thousand, even a few tens of thousands, of their funny little cars; it was almost like an extension of the Marshall Plan. But then two things happened. The first was that the numbers began to grow to the point where they were no longer funny, and some exporters became much more successful and well established. It's worth looking at the numbers of cars imported to the USA from other car manufacturing countries in 1959 and 1969:

From:	1959	1969
Britain	208,143	103,691
Germany	200,918	649,098
France	178,851	30,101
Italy	48,113	41,464
Sweden	26,075	45,191
Japan	2,696	218,109

It's not unfair to say, on the strength of these figures, that the UK and France had fallen well behind (the vast majority of those 1959 French imports had been Renault Dauphines, and the UK's remaining strength was mainly in MG and Triumph sports cars), West Germany had found out how to do it, Italy had never found out how to do it, and those quiet Swedes were doing rather well, while the Japanese, starting from almost nothing, were well on the way to showing what kind of steamroller force they would become throughout the 1970s. For the Americans, the point was that those 1969 imports came to well over a million cars a year, on a steeply rising trend. They could no longer be laughed off, never mind ignored, but it was difficult to know what to do about them. What the figures meant was that millions of Americans were getting fed up with driving the obligatory ton and a half of chrome-decorated Detroit monster, even if they could afford the petrol. True, tens of millions of them were still very happy to, but by 1969, if you wanted to look chic and trendy in the USA, especially if you lived in California, you bought a neat import. More than anything else, of course, in those days you bought a Volkswagen Beetle, which was all those things and unfailingly reliable as well – and which was bolstered by one of the most consistently creative and imaginative advertising campaigns ever used to sell a car.

While Europeans valued economy, the Americans were buying ever larger cars with ever more power. This Ford Fairlane is typical of the trend in the 1960s, when so many American cars were powered by huge V8 engines to propel their increasing bulk. Most of these cars had a 'perimeter frame' chassis, so that removing the roof to create a big convertible, as in this case, was relatively easy – and popular with buyers, especially in the southern states.

The third thing which happened to rock the smooth-running boat of the American industry was the weather in Los Angeles. The city, set in a half-bowl of mountains facing into the prevailing wind from the Pacific Ocean, had always suffered something of a weather problem. The local Native Americans are supposed to have told Spanish missionaries and settlers in the sixteenth century that it would be a bad place to build a city because every so often, when the wind and temperature were at certain levels, the bowl would fill with smoke. Los Angeles was built there anyway and, sure enough, every so often the bowl would fill with smoke. But during the 1960s it began to fill more often, and the smoke began to smell bad, making noses and throats sore and dry, and lungs ache and cough. A yellow haze would hang over the entire city, sometimes for a whole week or more. This was smog – smoke plus fog – and eventually the scientists decreed that one of its main causes was the gas that was emitted from motor-car exhausts.

The problem was that while most of the gas was harmless enough, some of its constituents 'cooked' in the sunlight to form the yellow haze. When the weather conditions were right (or rather, wrong), with an onshore breeze and what the scientists called a 'temperature inversion' in the layers of air above the city, the haze became trapped in the Los Angeles bowl and became denser and denser. Soon, most people knew they could blame their breathing problems on three substances – unburned hydrocarbons, carbon monoxide and oxides of nitrogen – coming from the exhaust pipes of all those thousands of huge, powerful cars that clogged the city freeways. By the end of the 1960s, the first laws were in place requiring car manufacturers to make sure their new cars produced only small amounts of those three noxious emissions, even if it meant that cars were less powerful, more difficult to drive and less economical.

WHAT HAPPENED IN EUROPE

During the 1960s, the Europeans had no cause to share these growing American concerns. The best European companies had always had more of a feel for safety than their American counterparts – Volvo had fitted safety-belts to its cars since the 1950s, while Fiat, Mercedes and Renault had all begun crash-testing and applying safety lessons at about the same time – and a good few years remained before the Europeans became so concerned about exhaust emissions. They didn't even have to worry too much about imports. For a few years after the war (oddly enough, as it now seems) some Europeans were concerned about a possible flood of cheap American imports but, as we have already seen, American cars quickly grew to the point where they were all but unsaleable in Europe. There was no need for import duties to restrict their numbers: the price of heavily taxed petrol was quite sufficient. As for the Japanese, it is true that their numbers grew during the 1960s, but not so much as

From the 1950s onwards, the huge volume of uncontrolled exhaust emissions emerging from the tailpipes of cars like the one shown opposite began to create serious air quality problems. For geographic reasons, these became most obvious in Los Angeles, where afternoons like this one became all too common. Eventually, during the 1960s, the car makers were required to limit the volume of noxious gas produced by their vehicles – and from then on, those limits became ever tighter.

to cause any distress (except for a few far-sighted commentators). In 1959, the Japanese exported three – just *three* – cars to Europe; in 1969 the figure was 72,706. This was still only a tiny proportion of the market as a whole, and in any case most of the sales were in small 'neutral' countries, with Finland, Belgium and Norway the biggest takers by far. During the whole of 1969 just over 2,000 Japanese cars were sold in the UK, and a princely 627 in West Germany. It was the calm before the storm.

A Californian beach scene from the 1960s, complete with a patrolling airship in the middle distance: and in the foreground, two Volkswagen Beetles, the favourite transport of the Californian young. For them, the Beetle represented rebellion against traditional American values as represented by the two-ton 'gas guzzler' – but it also helped that the Beetle would survive hard use and minimal maintenance without complaint, and delivered good economy in exchange for its modest performance.

The Europeans spent the whole of the 1960s fighting each other, jockeying for position, bringing out new models, trying to keep up with the demands of a market in which the consumer's voice became stronger year by year. Until the mid 1950s, especially in the UK, new cars had been in such short supply that buyers were almost pathetically grateful to take delivery and regarded a few trifling faults as a natural part of the running-in process. In the 1960s it was no longer so. The British were encouraged to take a tougher line when the Consumers' Association decided to study new cars with the same cold-blooded efficiency that it applied to electric kettles and vacuum cleaners. Once *Motoring Which?* had appeared, neither the British industry nor British motoring journalism would ever be the same again. The very first edition of this slender quarterly created a near-riot when it picked the Volkswagen Beetle as its 'Best Buy'. Why? Because almost nothing went wrong with it in 12,000 miles of testing, and overall it seemed to offer the best value for money. Suddenly, reliability took its rightful place alongside performance, equipment and stylishness as one of the criteria by which buyers judged their cars (in the USA it had always been taken for granted, which is why so many European exports failed after a first deceptive flush of success).

The main European concern, however, was to produce enough cars for a rapidly expanding market. Once again, it's worth looking at the bare figures (for production to the nearest 10,000 cars) which reflect ten years of evolution:

Country	1959	1969	Increase
UK	1,190,000	1,720,000	45%
France	1,130,000	2,170,000	92%
Germany	1,500,000	3,310,000	121%
Italy	471,000	1,480,000	214%
Sweden	96,000	243,000	153%

The immediate (and correct) conclusion is that the UK had lost its way, while Germany had become overwhelmingly Europe's industry leader with France in second place, and even Italy fast catching up (which it did, not many years later). The question is, how did it happen?

A great deal of the answer is found in the history of BMC and the way it planned its products. As pointed out earlier, during the 1960s BMC planned to unleash a series of 'grown-up Minis' to hit the market for small and medium-sized cars. Its first effort was a great success. The 1100, launched as a Morris, then badge-engineered into an Austin, an MG, a Riley, a Wolseley, and eventually a Vanden Plas, was neatly styled by Pininfarina, roomy in relation to its size and weight, comfortable thanks to Alex Moulton's 'Hydrolastic' rubber-and-fluid suspension, and had the same reassuring stability and handling as the Mini itself. It easily became the UK's best-selling series of cars. The obvious next thing to do was to grow the car by about as much again, to create a replacement for the Morris Oxford/Austin Cambridge and their badge-brothers. This time it all went badly wrong. The car that emerged as the Austin 1800 was too big, too heavy and too expensive for its logical purpose. It was also ugly, and it flopped.

Part of the reason for this failure could be found at Ford. In 1961 the company launched its riposte to the success of the Mini, and it was completely unexpected. Instead of a 'clever' car, it emerged as a ruthlessly optimized conventional car that had been designed after years of careful consumer research, overseen by a man who later went on to head Ford of Britain, Terry (later Sir Terence) Beckett. The new

The first 'big Mini' from BMC was the 1100/1300 series. This roomy and economical model enjoyed great success and was Britain's best-selling car for a number of years. However, BMC's devotion to 'badge-engineering' was such that the company also offered it with no fewer than six name badges: Austin, Morris, MG, Riley, Wolseley and Vanden Plas. They might have done much better spending the money to create a hatchback version; this is the 2-door MG 1300.

Instead of creating the next 'big Mini' model one step up from the 1100/1300, BMC deliberately avoided direct confrontation with the Ford Cortina and introduced the 1800. Extremely strong, cavernous inside, but huge and unwieldy by the standards of its day, the 1800 was a commercial failure (as the 18/85). No wonder everyone seems more interested in the bowsprit of HMS Victory!

model was christened the Consul Cortina, but before long it became simply the Cortina, and through being visibly 'more car for the money', it chased the BMC 1100 hard for that best-seller spot in the charts. It had a profound effect on BMC Chairman George Harriman, who decreed that no new BMC product should compete head-on with the Cortina. If the Oxford/Cambridge replacement had been sensibly sized, it would have done; and so it ended up larger, and much too big for its intended market. Indeed, the Morris Oxford was made to soldier on to fill the gap, long past its sell-by date, finally expiring only in 1971. Even the Mini itself suffered from floundering product management, appearing first as the awful Riley Elf/Wolseley Hornet with a 'stuck-on' boot extension, and then as the Clubman with a new, longer, angular nose which completely spoiled its pert looks.

BMC also made errors in its big-car programme (see Chapter Four), and in 1969 crowned a disastrous decade with the launch of the Maxi, intended to be what the 1800 should have been, and probably one of the most underdeveloped cars ever to be foisted on an unsuspecting public – although by that time, suspicions really should have been aroused. As it was, one distinguished motoring journalist likened operating its five-speed gearchange to 'stirring a knitting needle in a bag of marbles'. His colleagues wished they had thought of so accurate and evocative a description.

Above *The Ford Cortina, in its original Mark I form, simple but good value – and profitable for its manufacturer.*

Below *The Riley Elf, a badge-engineered Mini with an added tail to spoil its classic simplicity.*

By that time, it seemed hardly to matter that BMC management appeared to have lost its grip and that militant trade unions seemed to be running the factories, with productivity and quality steadily falling.

Ford, meanwhile, turned the screw of BMC's discomfort with a completely updated Cortina Mark 2 in 1966, and followed by replacing the Anglia with the Escort in 1968. Leaving aside its disastrous Mark 4 Zephyr/Zodiac series of 1966 (see Chapter Four), Ford could apparently do little wrong in the 1960s, even though at that time it never ventured into front-wheel

The Hillman Imp. Intended as a rival for the Mini but arriving in the market five years later, the outwardly pretty Imp was condemned to failure from the start. Built – by job-creating government order – in a brand-new factory 300 miles from the main Rootes Group base in Coventry, its early production was plagued by technical problems which resulted in a terrible reliability record. Worse still, it used a rear-mounted engine just when the rest of Europe had decided the Mini formula worked best. The slightly strange angle of this car's front wheels betrays the unusual front suspension arrangement intended to alleviate rear-engine handling and stability problems.

drive. Vauxhall adopted the same approach but never succeeded. Its best car of the 1960s was surely the little Viva; the medium-sized Victor never shook off the poor start of its initial 1958 version, and was crucified by *Motoring Which?* on more than one occasion. The big Cresta (see Chapter Four) also failed to make any impact. It was no surprise when, during the 1970s, General Motors transferred all its European car engineering development to Opel, leaving Vauxhall simply as the manufacturer of its own badge-engineered Opel models.

Yet the real sufferer of the 1960s was the Rootes Group, which had staked everything on a Mini rival, the Imp. The Imp was pretty, but that was where its virtues seemed to stop. It was rear-engined, and so suffered the inevitable stability and handling problems of that layout. It was very ambitiously engineered, with (for example) a completely new all-aluminium overhead camshaft engine developed by Coventry Climax. With the benefit of hindsight, it was far too ambitious to avoid teething troubles in production, even though it was delayed until the Mini had enjoyed a four-year start in the market. Worst of all, the government (a Conservative government, it should be recalled) decreed that Rootes could not build its new factory where it wanted to, near Coventry, but that it should create jobs in Scotland by building its new plant at Linwood on the outskirts of Glasgow. In exactly the same way, the government forced BMC to build its new commercial vehicle plant at Bathgate, between

A year or so before the Imp was announced, Renault replaced its rear-engined 4CV with a new R4, front-driven and utilitarian in the extreme. Outwardly little more than a tin shed on wheels, with a price to match, the R4 proved remarkably tough as well as being safe, economical and comfortable. It remained in production for over 30 years, and over 5 million examples were made, including the fourgonette van versions beloved of the French Post Office and almost every self-employed artisan in France.

Glasgow and Edinburgh. Both projects failed miserably, and by the early 1980s the Rootes plant at Linwood, from which the first car emerged only in 1963, had already been bulldozed. Rootes could not survive and was bought out by Chrysler, then seeking to establish a greater European presence to rival Ford and General Motors; but by the end of the 1970s, Chrysler in turn had sold its European factories to Peugeot.

As for Triumph, it seemed to have the makings of moderate success. After the 2000 it produced only one other genuinely new car during the 1960s, the front-driven – but rather oddly engineered – 1300; but it tweaked and shuffled its existing engines, chassis and bodyshells to end up with an attractive range. It came as no great surprise when Triumph, headed by Donald Stokes and encouraged by the government, effectively took over the physically much larger BMC after the latter had run into terminal problems at the end of the 1960s. Sadly, as we now know, the resulting British Leyland didn't fare very much better.

In France, while all this was going on, most of the real running was being made by Renault. In 1961 the company launched its boxy 'tin shed' R4, with front-wheel drive. The R4 was in many ways crude and utilitarian (though not to the extent of the Citroën 2CV) but it was cheap and reliable, and eventually it was made in its millions, lasting into the 1990s. Renault replaced the fragile Dauphine with the tougher, more angular R8 and R10, still rear-engined, but followed with another front-driven masterpiece, the medium-sized R16, arguably the world's first 'proper' hatchback design (as opposed to an estate car) and supremely comfortable into the bargain. At the very end of the decade Renault launched the R12, again front-driven but in many respects Renault's interpretation of the philosophy behind the Ford Cortina. The next real Renault master-stroke, the cute little R5, would follow in 1972.

While all this was going on Citroën suffered, trying to maintain its increasingly shaky position, knowing it would have nothing really new and exciting to offer until 1970 when, in what seems like a stroke of total mismanagement, it launched brand-new models – the big SM sports coupé and the medium-sized, high-technology GS – within six months of each other. The strain eventually proved too much and Michelin was forced to sell Citroën to Peugeot. That canny company, thanks to a prudent management which always retained a clear view of where it was headed, was by that time strong enough to absorb the culture shock of becoming responsible for Citroën and pressed ahead to become a power in the industry. Throughout the 1960s, Peugeot achieved two notable launches, one the front-driven 204, immortalized for the British market by the unforgettably misjudged advertising punch-line ('But it's got rubber mats, darling'), and the other the tough and worthy – but mainly conventional – 405. Simca survived the decade despite its ill-judged rear-engined 1000, but thanks to its later front-driven 1100, engineered with more than a little help from Fiat (there were some strange backstairs politics going on in the European industry at this time). Ultimately Chrysler sold Simca, together with the former Rootes Group, to Peugeot. Peugeot tried, but mainly failed, to create a third marque out of the Chrysler interest, christening it Talbot – but that was a story mainly of the 1980s.

Meanwhile in Germany, as the figures indicate, most things went well but not all of them did. Mercedes went from strength to strength, but deserves more discussion in Chapter Four. BMW, having flirted closely with oblivion, was rescued in 1961 by one brilliant design, the 'New Class' 1500 which formed the engineering foundation for the company's entire product range for many years to come. With a simple but powerful and reliable 1.5-litre engine which would 'stretch' to 1.8 litres, an effective but not too expensive all-independent suspension, and a body that was light but stiff, and attractively styled, the 1500 and then the 1800 started BMW on the road towards the big league.

Volkswagen, however, was in trouble – not that one would have guessed it from the production figures. After all, in 1959, Volkswagen made 605,301 cars – all Beetles, in effect – and exported around 200,000 of them to the USA. In 1969 the company made 1,531,651 cars (and 107,979 commercial vehicles, most of them the ubiquitous Microbus) and exported nearly 600,000 of them to the USA. The numbers, however, were not central to the argument. What everyone wanted to know was what would happen after the Beetle. True, it was probably one of the greatest motoring success stories of the middle of the twentieth century, but it had been designed in the 1930s and could not go on for ever. Volkswagen remained, in effect, a single-model company and there were fears as to what might happen if demand for the

Beetle suddenly fell away as it began to be seen as old-fashioned. After all, the Beetle was rear-engined, and it was beginning to be renowned not only for its reliability and its 'unburstable' flat-out cruising (at around 70mph!) but also for its waywardness in sidewinds and its tricky handling in some cornering situations. Newer cars also beat it for roominess and luggage space.

The company tried to re-body the Beetle and turn it into the slightly larger 1500, without much success. It followed with the all-new 411, a much bigger car that determinedly, and mistakenly, stuck to the same formula of a rear-mounted air-cooled engine. It flopped. It took over the small but innovative NSU, which had fallen into financial straits following its over-ambitious launch of the Wankel-engined Ro80, and tried to turn NSU's follow-up design, the front-driven K70, into a Volkswagen design. Again, the market didn't really want to know. All the time, studies were being pursued on an amazingly advanced, almost certainly over-ambitious new car with a 'flat' engine in the centre, beneath the floor. The uncertainty only ended with the announcement of the first Golf, in 1974. Up to that time, the motoring world always wondered quite what would become of Volkswagen, however big it had grown.

Another step eventually taken by Volkswagen was to buy Audi, the former Auto-Union, from its brief partnership with Mercedes. Audi certainly had the front-drive expertise that Volkswagen desperately needed, but it was a distinct range, which was beginning to do quite well in its own right, and the VW management had the sense not to try to absorb it completely. As for the American-owned companies in Germany, the picture was almost the reverse of that in the UK. General Motors' Opel was easily the second biggest German manufacturer in terms of numbers, and doing very well without being technically ambitious, while Ford was having much more of a struggle and had no star model with the stature of the Cortina.

Then there was Italy – which, more and more, came to mean Fiat. The Turin company took over its neighbour Lancia in 1967 and tried to maintain the Lancia image while beginning, slowly, to rationalize the engineering; but you could still buy a 'real' Lancia, especially the lovely Fulvia, well into the 1970s. Fiat itself was more concerned with its own product range, producing the front-engined, rear-driven 124 which was very much an 'Italian Cortina', simple in design, light and efficient, and a lot of car for the money (when, eventually, Fiat replaced the 124, it did a deal with the Russians and turned over the entire inventory to equip a huge new factory, named Togliattigrad in honour of the leader of the Italian Communist party).

State-owned Alfa Romeo steered clear of the small-car market (or were steered clear of it under pressure from Fiat; in the Alfa Romeo museum there is a little jewel of a prototype 'mini-Giulietta', the Tipo 104, complete with a twin-cam engine of only 850cc, which never saw production). Alfa's great success story throughout the whole of the 1960s was the growing Giulia series: most of those concerned would probably rather forget about the bigger 2600. The 1750, which was a stretched, 'grown-up' Giulia, and the Alfasud, were to be the stories for the 1970s.

That, of course, leaves the Japanese. For them, the 1960s were the decade in which they laid the foundations for their subsequent huge expansion. As already related, in 1959 Japan exported 3 cars to Europe and 2,696 to the USA. This was out of a total production of just 78,598. By 1969, the equivalent figures were 72,706 cars exported to Europe, and 218,109 to the USA, out of 2,611,499 cars produced. By then the giants Toyota and Nissan were already establishing their credentials, while Honda was beginning seriously to turn its attentions from motor cycles to cars. Ten years after that, we would all be very well aware of the results . . .

In the UK, at the end of the 1960s, the future of the motor industry still seemed full of hope. The Mini had emerged as an epoch-making design and its larger cousin the BMC 1100 was the country's best-selling model. The Ford Cortina was selling strongly and had just been joined by the smaller Escort. By far the larger proportion of cars sold in the UK were still made in the UK. What few people foresaw was that the 1970s would be a decade of disaster, especially for the companies that had just drawn together to form British Leyland. A combination of weak and incompetent management on that front, plus a move away from Mini-sized cars towards medium-sized family cars, meant it would be Ford who profited most, as the Cortina became the best-seller. And to cap it all, the politicians would remove almost all restraints on the British car market, in a way that sucked in huge numbers of imports and paved the way for the British industry to hit its lowest ebb during the 1980s. In 1969, all that was in the future – and to be fair, it would have taken a very clear crystal ball to see it coming.

CHAPTER THREE

SPORTS CARS

*T*HE BRITISH ARE CONVINCED they invented the sports car. Both the French and the Italians would argue with that, and can point to a whole series of 1930s classics of their own as evidence. It is far more accurate to say that the British invented the cheap, simple sports car, and that was mainly due to the vision of Cecil Kimber who created MG in 1927 (which originally stood for Morris Garages) to build light two-seaters whose price was kept low through the use of standard Morris parts, especially the engines and gearboxes. By international standards the early MGs were technically backward and not very fast, but they looked the part and that mattered much more. As the shadow of the Great Depression began to subside, the 1930s became the decade of the bright young things, of well-off young men and their glamorous girlfriends, zooming about – to general parental disapproval, no doubt – in their neat little sports cars. Though the P-series (and later the larger T-series) MGs were in the majority, other British makers were quick to copy the formula. A good many of the small pre-war sports cars which are MGs to the untutored eye turn out, on closer inspection, to be Rileys, or Singers, or any of several others. There were bigger and more powerful sports cars, of course, but these were built in small numbers for the very rich, in the UK as in other places.

As is so often the case, the legend of the bright young things in their sports cars has become much magnified. The sum total of MG production from the late 1920s up to 1939 was around 22,500 cars. If you add the Riley Imps and the Singer Le Mans and other makes, Britain's immediate pre-war population of 'little sports cars' might have been around 40,000 at most. It just goes to show how few bright young things there really were in a country of 50 million – at two to a car, barely enough to fill Wembley Stadium – or perhaps it goes to show how mobile and energetic that handful were, how much publicity they attracted, and how other people aspired to be like

The Austin-Healey 3000 was always considered something of a brute of a car, hard work to drive quickly with its heavy steering, clutch and gearchange, and not terribly comfortable. But it could be driven quickly, as its success in major rallies proved – even if the BMC works team cars were always run on raised suspension to enable them to survive on rough roads. The 3-litre, six-cylinder engine delivered more than enough power to give the car performance to match its looks.

them. However, the MG models did something that the others could not manage: they survived the war.

Their survival had nothing to do with the home market. During the war, they were a favourite vehicle for young British officers, many of whom had bought them in happier times and who were now almost the only people who could afford to – and were allowed to – keep them on the road between 1939 and 1945. A lot of British-based American servicemen had also seen and admired these sports cars so there was a ready market for them on the other side of the Atlantic when hostilities ended. Because MG was part of the massive Nuffield Organization, and because the post-war British motor industry went into 'export or die' mode, that market was exploited for all it was worth. A slightly modified T series, the TC, was put back into production and, before long, the famous MG works at Abingdon was producing over three times as many cars as it ever had before 1939. Around 80 per cent of these cars were exported, mostly to the USA.

It was a splendid export earner, but it could not last for ever. For the average American driver, the T-series MGs were little more than toys. They were certainly not capable of withstanding the wear and tear of American driving and American road surfaces without skilled and careful servicing, and mostly they didn't get it. British exporters in the early post-war years were much keener on selling than on providing technical backup. It was a deficiency that killed other British cars in the US market very quickly, but the sports MGs were being sold to enthusiasts. They were more tolerant – but they weren't by any means infinitely tolerant.

In any case, things were about to change. Even in the sentimental market for sports cars, you couldn't go on building the same product for ever. MG, shortly to become part of the giant BMC, knew it had to replace the TF, the last of its 'traditional' designs. Its hand was forced not least by the upstart Triumph, which had already launched the more modern TR2 that was busy carving itself a slice of the rich US market. In an altogether higher league, Jaguar's XK120 had already established the accepted look for modern sports cars.

MG responded with a car that looked much more different than it really was, the MGA. This had a smooth, all-enveloping body that took its cues from Jaguar, from Triumph and even, some thought, from Alfa Romeo. Beneath the new skin, most of the mechanical parts were still borrowed from the BMC saloon car range but, once again, that didn't matter. The MGA was a success, destined to be built in bigger numbers than any previous MG.

At about this time, however, towards the end of the 1950s, BMC did something daring and imaginative. For all its mechanical simplicity, the MGA (and its successor the MGB, launched in 1962) was no longer small or cheap. With the help of sports

Below *The MG T-series was replaced by the MGA, which in turn gave way in the early 1960s to the MGB seen here. Despite the much more modern and roomier body, the wheels are still wire-spoked with knock-on hubs; the white-wall tyres were strictly for the American market which more or less insisted on them at the time. The background is formed by the first prototype Vickers VC10, apparently being made ready for its first flight from Brooklands in June 1962.*

Opposite *While the MG T-series eventually grew to be replaced by the MGA and MGB, BMC recaptured the spirit of the original P-series MGs with the Austin-Healey Sprite: ultra-compact, very simple, using as many standard parts as possible and extremely cheap in relation to the amount of fun it offered. The original Sprite design seen here became known as the 'frog-eye', for obvious reasons. Later series were more conventional in appearance, and the Sprite was joined by its sister-ship the MG Midget. Early sales promotion of the Sprite* (left) *leaned heavily on the notion of fun, though in truth you had to be agile to get in and out when the hood was up.*

car specialist Donald Healey, BMC management relaunched the idea of the cheap, simple sports car, compact and fun to drive, an equivalent of the 1930s P-type. The new car would have the 1-litre A-series engine from the Morris Minor, rather than the 1.5-litre B-series from the medium-sized saloons.

The new small sports car emerged as the Austin-Healey Sprite, later joined by its close relative the MG Midget. They made driving fun again: not very comfortable, but reasonably cheap and entertaining. The cars were cheap because they were very simple. The first 'frog-eye' Sprite didn't even have a boot lid – you tipped the seats forward and loaded it from inside – and, for a long time, you had to stop and open the bonnet to turn the heater on or off. They were fun because, being so small and simple, they were light enough for the small engine to give a decent performance (by the standards of the time). The chassis design was crude and the ride dreadfully uncomfortable, but the steering was quick and accurate and that mattered more to a keen young man.

One of the things achieved by the Sprite and Midget (inevitably, enthusiasts christened the two badge-engineered models the 'Spridget') was that, at last, it became respectable for women to drive sports cars, rather than travel decoratively in the passenger seat. It was not that it had never happened. A handful of 'fast ladies' had always kept up with the men, even in the most powerful cars. But until the advent of the 'Spridget', the sort of girl who drove her own sports car, an MGA or a Triumph TR3 perhaps, might be exciting and desirable but was also likely to be the kind of girl

Above **Underneath the sweeping lines of the Sunbeam Alpine lay most of the mechanical contents of the Hillman Minx family saloon. Note, yet again, the wire wheels and knock-on hubs which were an obligatory part of any 1960s sports car specification. For those who wanted real excitement, the Alpine formed the basis for the visually similar Sunbeam Tiger with a 'shoehorned' American V8 under the bonnet, providing performance which tended to outrun the capabilities of the chassis.**

who would worry any respectable young man's mother! The Spridget, because it was small and cuddly (especially the original 'frog-eye') and not terribly fast, became the first truly acceptable woman's sports car, the lively alternative to a dull small saloon. The other possible choice for a woman was, as we have already discussed, the Mini.

Not to be outflanked by BMC's move towards the small sports car, Triumph produced a Spridget rival in the form of the Spitfire, based on the Herald. Between them these models formed the bottom end of the sports car market, where margins were so slim that nobody else, except a handful of tiny manufacturers operating out of glorified work-shops rather than proper factories, was interested. There were many more competi-tors higher up the scale, where the MGA and then the MGB, and the Triumph TR series (already up to TR4 when the decade started), had rivals in the Sunbeam-Talbot Alpine, the Daimler Dart, the big and brutal Austin-Healey 3000 and, at the very top, the car that turned every head and also eliminated a number of potential rivals before they ever left the drawing-board: the Jaguar E-type.

Right **The Triumph TR sports series ran from the original TR2 to the final TR6. One of the major evolutions in its design came with the introduction of independent rear suspension on the TR4, to produce the TR4 IRS seen here; but throughout its life the TR remained a car to be treated with respect by drivers who wanted to avoid overdoses of excitement.**

Above **By degrees the original 'frog-eye' Sprite metamorphosed into the far more conventional car seen here – actually an MG Midget, but you needed to be something of an expert to tell it from the equivalent Austin-Healey Sprite unless you had a clear sight of the front grille. Inevitably the two 'badge-engineered' companion models were often referred to collectively as the Spridget.**

Left *Taking her for a spin – something of which the Austin-Healey 3000 was always capable if provoked. Exactly how the problem would have been solved in the proposed 4000GT version (abandoned once the Jaguar E-type had appeared) has never been made clear, but it would certainly have involved serious development work.*

The purest and most beautiful of lines, a shape which took the motoring world by storm when it appeared at the 1961 Geneva Motor Show: the Jaguar E-type. Not merely a pretty face, the E-type also offered a race-proved twin-cam six-cylinder engine, and a properly engineered independent rear suspension, so it behaved as well as it looked. Most rival engineering teams were as stunned by the (relatively) low cost of the car as they were by its sheer performance and all-round ability.

When it appeared at the Geneva Motor Show in March 1961, the E-type rewrote the rule book for big, powerful sports cars. Starting in 1948, Jaguar had already worked its way through the XK120, 140 and 150, cars that were hugely admired for their looks and their performance. But the E-type was everything these cars had been, and much more besides: looks to put even the Italians in the shade, and a truly modern chassis with proper independent rear suspension. To add to the sensation, the two leading motoring magazines, *The Autocar* and *The Motor*, ran road tests which reported a maximum speed of over 150mph. Much later, it emerged that these test cars had been very specially 'prepared', quite apart from running on non-standard tyres which would stand up to the speed, but it didn't matter – the image had been established. In true Jaguar tradition, the E-type offered its package at a price nobody else could match. It is known, for example, that BMC had an even bigger and more brutal Healey 4000GT on the stocks when the E-type appeared. But it would have

cost nearly twice as much, and as a result, it never saw the light of day. Instead the Healey itself was replaced by a 3-litre, six-cylinder MGC, but that proved to be a flop.

Some of these larger sports cars appealed to different kinds of people – either they were designed like that, or it happened by accident. The Alpine and the Dart looked the part but really they were 'semi-sports' cars, comfortable, well equipped and smart enough for well-off young women to be seen in (look for the Dart, and feel sorry for its unfortunate lady owner, in the classic Michael Caine film, *Get Carter*). The Triumph TR on the other hand, and even more so the 'big Healey', the 3000, were cars designed for men – although that did not stop Pat Moss (Stirling's sister) driving the Healey to great results in the Liège–Rome–Liège, one of Europe's longest and toughest rallies. The Jaguar E-type, for all its svelte looks, amazing performance and excellent handling, for some reason became widely known as the 'hairdressers'

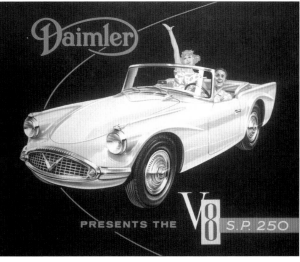

car', to the extent that some 'serious' drivers shied away from it. Perhaps, if it hadn't looked quite so sensational, or even if it had been more expensive, things would have been different.

The 1960s also produced some interesting British sports cars made in small numbers by specialized companies. Mainly they used bodies of glass-reinforced plastic (grp), which could be made without a huge investment in press tools for steel panels. Even the Daimler Dart used this kind of bodywork, but the newcomers included TVR of Blackpool, Reliant of Tamworth (who built the Sabre and Scimitar sports cars as a kind of diversion from their three-wheelers), Marcos from the West Country, Ginetta, and Gilbern, who built the Invader and claimed fame as the only Welsh car manufacturer.

To these were added Peter Morgan, whose Malvern factory carried on building the kind of cars it always had, using traditional designs and methods, and limiting the production rate to keep demand (and prices) strong. Morgan, in fact, carved a particular niche for itself in the world of the sports car. Family-run, often with families working for it – there was a time when three generations, grandfather, father and son, could be found on the payroll in Malvern – it could afford to ignore most modern trends, including the urge to grow. It had begun life building sporting three-wheelers (with two wheels at the front and one at the rear) but graduated to a 'proper' sports car, the Plus 4. Throughout the 1960s, and indeed up to the present day, Morgan has produced a genuine 1930s sports car with as few concessions as possible to modernity. True, during the 1960s it introduced a much more powerful version, the Plus 8 with a 3.5-litre V8 engine (and a noisy and uncomfortable car to drive as fast as it is capable of going). The company has even managed to preserve the character of its cars while building in the features, such as airbags, which are required by modern safety regulations.

The Daimler SP250, otherwise the Dart, was a slightly strange (especially for a company best known for products of solid dignity) but modestly successful attempt to offer a medium-sized sports car, powered by a compact 2.5-litre V8 engine. To avoid the heavy cost of tooling for a steel body, the SP250 was one of the pioneers of glass-reinforced plastic (grp) body construction. The car failed to survive Jaguar's takeover of Daimler but the engine lived on for some time in saloon cars.

The long-established Morgan, and the smaller British specialist newcomers had no equivalent in any other country. Most of the newcomers underwent various trials and tribulations, passing from crisis to financial crisis and from owner to owner, but they never gave up building interesting cars. TVR in particular survived in good shape, and went on to build cars which challenge for a place in the 'supercar' class (see Chapter Six). During the 1960s, though, it was interesting to note that with the exception of Morgan, most of these cars were 'hard-top' coupés, with hardly a folding hood in sight. It was the pointer to a trend.

BUT WHAT IS A SPORTS CAR, DADDY?

At about this time, part-way through the 1960s, a debate began that has never really been resolved: what exactly *is* a sports car? For years, people had thought they knew. A sports car had a distinctive and immediately recognizable appearance built around two seats, and a hood which could be lowered so that you could feel the wind in your hair. (For some girls in the 1960s, the ultimate test of a well-lacquered 'beehive' hairstyle was whether it remained intact when driven at 70mph in a Spridget!) Straight, flowing locks were temporarily out of fashion (besides, contrary to what most people think, the head-level wind in an open-topped car comes mainly from behind you). There was another problem besides: that fashion hallmark of the 1960s, the miniskirt, made it almost impossible to enter or leave a low-slung sports car with any kind of dignity. Eventually, the trouser suit provided the answer.

Returning to the basic question, enthusiasts when further pressed would also say that sports cars, being more powerful and lower-built than saloon cars, were faster and would go round corners quicker. The trouble was that, during the 1960s, this reassuring image began to fall apart. Saloon car racing became popular, and apart from being interesting and exciting, it also made it clear that modern saloons were extremely quick and handled very well. To make matters worse, the 1960s was the decade in which international rallying took on its modern form, making the transition from a navigational exercise to a series of races against the stop-watch along closed 'special stages' on unmade roads. It did not escape the attention of enthusiasts that the cars which did best in the new-style rallies were tough saloons, from Paddy Hopkirk's Mini-Cooper through Erik Carlsson's Saab 96 to Tom Trana's big Volvo Amazon. Traditional sports cars hurled along rough forest tracks usually ended up with their exhausts, transmissions and suspensions torn out. It wasn't just ground clearance which mattered, but the basic stiffness of a closed body, and the way it could be prepared to survive trouble.

All this was bad news for the traditional open-topped two-seater sports car, which went into a steady decline. More and more enthusiasts asked what was the point of buying something which, when exposed to the heat of competition, proved to be lacking. It didn't matter, of course, whether those people had any intention of indulging in competition themselves. In exactly the same way as (much later) most of the people who bought four-wheel-drive vehicles had no intention of indulging in serious off-road driving, they liked the idea that they could if they ever wanted to.

The manufacturers, sensing this mood, reacted in two ways. The first was to cease effective development of new 'soft-top' two-seaters, replacements for the MGB and the Triumph TR. In this they were encouraged, as the decade wore on, by the feeling that the new American safety regulations would eventually outlaw soft-top cars altogether – something which did not, in the event, happen. On a more positive front, the manufacturers began to cash in on the race and rally image by offering more powerful, specially equipped versions of their standard saloon cars. BMC was early into the field with the Mini Cooper and then the Mini Cooper S, the latter a car that really could make a sports car with twice as much power look very ordinary indeed. Ford quickly responded with the Cortina GT and then the Lotus-Cortina. Indeed, through as many seasons, ambitious club-level rally drivers seeking to remain competitive switched cars very much in unison: Cooper in 1962, Cortina GT in 1963, Cooper S in 1964, Lotus-Cortina in 1965. 'Proper' sports cars were forgotten. At the very end of the decade, *the* sporting car to have was probably a 'hot' Ford Escort, either the Twin Cam with Lotus-Cortina engine, or the fearsome sixteen-valve with the 1.6-litre Cosworth BDA engine, in effect a slightly detuned racing engine. It was a trend that in later years led to the 'hot-hatch' market, to the distress of the insurance companies.

Some designers and product planners took a different view of the sports car scene. For them, the essence of the sports car was not so much the wind in the hair, but rather the pleasure of driving, and the pride of ownership. They did not see a rock-hard ride and a leaky folding roof as a necessary part of the formula. Appearance was the thing: long-nosed, short-tailed, purposeful, with a sloping 'coupé' roof line which spoke of performance while concealing the fact that the back seat, while not generous, would take two children in comfort and two adults with a squeeze. It was a trend that extended even to existing sports cars: for many people, by far the most elegant version of the MGB was the hard-topped MGB GT introduced in 1965.

Ford led the way into this new concept, in the USA and Europe. In the USA, engineers 'raided the parts bin' – especially the bin full of Falcon saloon parts – and in 1964 came up with the original Mustang. It was done very quickly, with a small team, and consequently cost very little to develop, unlike the Edsel which at that time was still a recent and painful memory for

The Ford Mustang was a phenomenon. Its rapid development, using readily available parts, strangely echoed the origins of MG but the car was very different: light, powerful, long-nosed and short-tailed, it ushered in the era of the 'muscle car' in the USA. It was also amazingly successful, selling more units in its first year than any previous Ford model. This is the car close to its original 1964 launch form; several generations later, the name continues.

The Lotus Cortina (above), **powered by the twin-cam engine from the Lotus Elan, would outrun many sports cars of its day while seating four in comfort; the Triumph Spitfire** (below) **shared nothing with the famous fighter aircraft other than the name, despite the advertising hype.**

Ford. Even less like the Edsel, the Mustang was a stunning sales success, so much so that for a whole year the factories could not match the demand. The key to this success was a car which was light, simple, but with the raw power of a big V8 engine – and, of course, that eager, long-nosed look which came to characterize the 'muscle car'. The Mustang was a firm favourite even before Steve McQueen immortalized it on the streets of San Francisco during the chase scene in the film *Bullitt.* Thirty years and many versions later, Mustangs are still made. General Motors couldn't leave this market all to Ford, and developed its Mustang rivals, the Chevrolet Camaro and the Pontiac Firebird, to run alongside the big, beautiful but specialized, low-volume Chevrolet Corvette, the nearest thing there was in the 1960s to a real American sports car.

Meanwhile, in Britain, Ford set out to build on the sporting success it had already enjoyed with the Cortina GT, and then the Lotus Cortina. In 1968 it created what amounted to a small-scale Mustang, and called it the Capri – 'the car you always promised yourself'. The Capri did well enough in Europe, and especially in the UK, to become a legend in its own modest way. It was steadily improved through its production life, and enthusiasts will tell you that the last of the line, the Capri 2.8i, was also the best. For all that, Ford used the lighter and nimbler Escort for serious rallying, in the capable hands of the late Roger Clark and others. The lesson was that if you wanted to win at top level, you used your most suitable car, not your best-looking one.

ANSWERS TO CRUDITY

One criticism the enthusiasts justifiably levelled at most of the surviving 1960s sports cars was that however good they looked, underneath they were fairly crude, with axles and springs from the 1950s. True, the Jaguar E-type was superbly engineered, but attempts to create independent rear suspension arrangements without spending too much money often ended in tears. The Triumph Spitfire, for example, carried over the disastrous Herald swing-axle rear suspension – not unlike that of the Volkswagen Beetle in its general arrangement – that would lift and flick the tail if the driver was too ambitious, or just plain careless. Later in the decade, Triumph modified the Spitfire rear suspension (and even more vitally, that of its powerful 2-litre derivative the GT6) to improve the handling. Yet at the same time the company added independent rear suspension to the TR4, and ended up with a different set of handling problems for the unwary driver. The system was continued through the TR5 and the broad-mouthed TR6; but for the completely new TR7 of the 1970s, Triumph (or rather British Leyland, as it had then become)

Decidedly Lotus

The '2S 130 is as distinctive as the people who drive it. People sympathetic to the maxim that when one travels, one should travel in style. The suave, elegant lines, the bold colour styling, the luxuriously appointed interior - all are unmistakably Lotus. But handsome looks alone did not make our name one of legend ... the remarkable acceleration, the breath-taking performance (the new optional 5-speed gear box gives even smoother, quieter motorway cruising), the matchless handling and the unequalled road holding ... all are a part of the magic of the '2S 130. Add to these the life-saving glass fibre body construction, and you have - as Autocar put it '... a relaxed high-speed cruiser, with the race-bred drivers car only a gearchange away'. Take a test drive soon, and find out why Lotus are winning the world over. Write or talk to Harry Carter, (General Manager Marketing) Lotus Cars Ltd., Norfolk, NOR 92W. Tel: Wymondham 3411

Above: *The Lotus Elan Plus 2 was an extension of the Elan theme, launched by Lotus in 1967. Sharing much of the smaller car's engineering but with a larger and more spacious body able to house two children on a tiny bench back seat, it enabled families to extend their Lotus-driving period by several years. Quite what the young lady in yellow thinks of the idea is not clear.*

Previous page *The Triumph Spitfire was derived from the Herald saloon as a rival for the Austin-Healey Sprite and MG Midget. The Spitfire 1500 was the final version, with the engine 'stretched' to 1.5-litre capacity. By this time the Spitfire rear suspension had been modified to cure the car's previous wayward handling.*

reverted to a 'live' rear axle! As for the MGs, no serious attempt was made to bring their chassis engineering into the second half of the twentieth century. Plenty of perceptive people in the 1960s saw the MGB for what in effect it was: a short-wheelbase version of the Austin Cambridge with a cramped two-seater body. Today, the rose-tinted spectacles of retrospection blur the view.

But the enthusiasts couldn't criticize the Lotus Elan, designed and developed by Colin Chapman. Chapman, trained like so many sports car enthusiasts in the aircraft industry, set up Lotus Cars in a small way in Hornsey, North London, then moved further out to Cheshunt, and eventually to a purpose-built factory – on the edge of the old Hethel airfield, which served as a test track – in Norfolk. His genius gave the Elan, by way of a stiff chassis and an excellent suspension system, steering and handling which are still admired today. It's worth noting that he achieved these results without resorting to wheels and tyres of enormous width, all too common today. Chapman paid Harry Mundy, one of the best independent engineers in Britain, to design a new twin-cam cylinder head for the Ford Cortina engine, to give the Elan performance to match its cornering ability (Chapman offered Mundy a straight £100 or £1 an engine; Mundy took the £100, and eventually saw production of the Twin Cam run well past the 10,000 mark!).

The Elan was much more practical than the Elite which had preceded it – the Elite had a mostly plastic body and a tiny, vivid but temperamental Coventry Climax engine. True, the Elan was considerably more expensive than the MGs and Triumphs with which it was so often compared, but it was far more capable. After the Elan, and still in the 1960s, Chapman followed up with the 'grown up' Elan Plus 2, which was longer, wider, and with a back seat of sorts. But the Plus 2 was a hard-top, never made with a folding hood: even Colin Chapman had abandoned the traditional image of the sports car, although one of his earliest designs, the tiny and spartan Lotus Seven, was taken up by Caterham Cars, which still builds modestly up-dated versions with great success. Lotus Cars itself, meanwhile, moved from the Elan and the Plus 2 to the heavier, faster Esprit, much more expensive and a contender for 'supercar' status.

The Lotus Elan, like some of its contemporaries, was also designed to exploit a peculiarity of the British market, the demand for 'kit cars'. For several years, car buyers were exempt from purchase tax – which at that time was considerable – if they bought their cars as complete kits of parts and assembled them themselves. It was a concession that created a number of problems. Lotus ran an inspection service for customer-assembled kit cars, and reckoned that many of them were downright dangerous as presented, needing a lot of work to put them right (the *Motoring Which?* car test unit built and assembled an Elan, took it – incognito, of course – for its check, and were not only complimented on the quality of their build, but regaled with horror stories about the state of some of the cars which had come to Chesham!). Eventually, with the advent of VAT, the 'kit car' market was brought to an end, probably to the relief of most people in the trade.

By the end of the 1960s, the traditional image of the sports car was in full retreat. MGBs and Triumph TRs were still in production but apart from the ill-starred TR7, which was a thoroughly cynical exercise in giving the American market a sports car without spending too much, there were no replacements. The existing cars soldiered on, the MGs in particular made ugly with the addition of huge 'rubber' bumpers to meet the latest American safety regulations, until eventually the order was issued to close down and sell the Abingdon factory. The 1960s projects which might have saved MG, from a mid-engined replacement for the MGB to a tiny Midget replacement with a front-drive Mini Cooper power pack, were all shelved.

What was happening in the rest of Europe while all this was going on? Sadly, not a great deal, although just enough to provide a spur for the British manufacturers. The French had entirely lost their enthusiasm for the sports car. They were far too busy turning out cheap little cars for the masses. France had no small, specialist builders of the kind who had managed to establish themselves, if not actually to prosper, in the UK. In Italy, smaller companies had sprung up (or been resurrected after the war) but for the most part they concentrated on building very powerful, very expensive cars, not sports cars by any reasonable definition but what came to be known as 'supercars' (see Chapter Six). The only compact sports cars at a reasonable price came from Alfa Romeo and Fiat. Alfa produced the Giulietta 1300 and Giulia 1600 Spider – Spider having become a generic Italian term for a car with a folding hood. Later in the decade, they gave way to the bigger 1750 Spider. The bodies came from Bertone or Pininfarina. Compared with their British rivals the Alfa Romeos were expensive, but they had much better engines – twin-cam, naturally – and well-developed chassis with excellent handling. Alfa Romeo never considered building a smaller sports car, a rival for the Sprite and Midget.

Fiat, on the other hand, had a small sports car of sorts. After creating the dumpy rear-engined 850 saloon, they commissioned Bertone to create a Spider version of it, while themselves designing the neat little 805 Coupé. These two cars were attractive, and because they were small and low-powered it didn't greatly matter that the engine was at the wrong end. Fiat also widened the appeal of its new 124, launched in 1966, by adding both Sport Spider and Coupé versions. The Sport Spider, styled and built by Pininfarina, was to enjoy a very long production life indeed; the Coupé, styled by Fiat themselves, emerged as an extremely pretty car which many people thought was 'uglified' by two successive 'facelifts'. The 124 Coupé, unlike the 124 Spider, was exported to Britain with some success, although before long it faced a tough home-grown competitor in the Ford Capri.

In Germany, meanwhile, the 1960s saw the emergence of a true phenomenon, in the shape of the Porsche 911. The previous Porsche model, the 356, had owed a great deal to the Volkswagen Beetle (designed by Ferdinand Porsche, of course) but the 911 – which would have been the 901, until somebody pointed out that Peugeot had registered all the three-figure numbers with an 0 in the middle – was an all-new design, though it still had its engine slung aft of the rear axle, and the next thirty years were to be spent in trying to tame the wayward handling that resulted. That did not stop the 911 from becoming one of the all-time classic designs, tainted only by the unfortunate image it gained in the British market, during the boom years of the 1980s, as the 'yuppie special', the only possible choice for the suddenly rich young.

One of the strengths of the Porsche 911 was the way its flat-six engine could be 'stretched' – made bigger and bigger, and more and more powerful, without altering the whole design. The original 2-litre engine was opened out by degrees to 2.2, 2.4, 2.7 and eventually a full 3 litres. Every time power was added, the 911 became in some ways even more of an 'expert's car', but that just added to its appeal. On the other hand, this growth soon took the 911 out of the sports-car bracket altogether, and made it something more nearly approaching the 'supercars' (see Chapter Six). The process was effectively completed when the first 911 Turbo was announced in the early 1970s. Along the way, though, the 911 introduced another fashion in the form of the 'Targa' top, an alternative to the folding hood, in which part of the roof was formed by a stiff panel that could be locked in place, or removed and stowed in the boot. The Targa top, in various forms, became popular on later sporting cars from several manufacturers.

Because the 911 grew up so fast, becoming more expensive in the process, there was pressure on Porsche to produce something cheaper. Towards the end of the 1960s the company obliged with the 914, a mid-engined (and therefore in theory, more technically advanced) model which appeared in two versions, one with a flat-four Volkswagen engine, and the other, the 914/6, with a 2-litre Porsche flat-six. Sadly, the 914 never caught on. Unlike the 911, it wasn't particularly good-looking. Also, it wasn't very practical suffering, as it did, from all the drawbacks of the mid-engine layout – poor luggage space, awkward engine access, and a noisy cabin. Worst of all, however, having been created as the 'people's Porsche' or *VolksPorsche*, it found itself being referred to as the VoPo, which was also the German slang shorthand for the hated East German political police force. Porsche persisted with a 914 for a few years and then gave up to concentrate again on the 911.

A potential rival for the small British sports cars of the 1960s was the 'high-tech' Honda S600/800 series. Only the S800 was offered for sale in Britain, but at a price too high to compete successfully with the Sprite and Midget. Its performance was exceptional for such a small engine, but the Japanese still had a lot to learn about handling and ride comfort.

In Japan, there were stirrings of an interest in sports cars – the Japanese were interested in almost anything with four wheels and an engine. Very early in its extension from motor cycle to car making, Honda had produced some exquisite small sports cars, one of which – the S800 – was exported to Britain. The S800 was Spridget-sized but with the most amazingly high-tech engine (though sadly, without a chassis to match). But the company failed to follow up on this early promise, and for many years the front-runner among Japanese sports-car makers was Datsun (which became Nissan). Datsun created a series of models known as Fairlady in Japan and some other parts of the world, but referred to as the 240Z when it finally arrived in Britain during the early 1970s. Eventually, twenty years later, it was the Japanese who reignited the sports car market with one new design, the Mazda MX5.

As for the Americans, their 'big three' manufacturers knew what kind of car would sell in large numbers. They were aware that it would certainly not be a small and delicate sports car in the European tradition but instead a convertible version of their 'muscle cars', the Ford Mustang, the Chevrolet Camaro, and the Dodge Dart. General Motors, Ford and Chrysler knew they were leaving the door open for a steady trickle of imports from Europe, but it wouldn't have been worth their while spending money on developing that kind of car, even if they could have been sure of getting it right. Already, the huge difference between American and European fuel prices was beginning to have its effect even on the sports car scene. For most

MORGAN MOTOR COMPANY LIMITED
MALVERN LINK • WORCESTERSHIRE • WR14 2LL • ENGLAND
TELEPHONE: MALVERN (0684) 573104/5 • FACSIMILE: (0684) 892295

Americans, a sports car was something with the performance of a big V8 engine, and that was something few Europeans, and even fewer Japanese, could contemplate. Certainly it's unfair to criticize the Americans, as Europeans sometimes do, for their apparent disinterest in 'proper' sports cars. The Americans built for their market, which they knew extremely well.

In the UK, once the 1960s had ended, the sports car tradition was kept alive mainly by the smaller specialists. The larger manufacturers, led by British Leyland, decided it was too expensive to develop a car for such a small market, and that it was easier to coax the young enthusiast towards the 'hot hatch'. Before long there was a kind of revolution among buyers which meant that the hot hatches, cars like the Ford Escort, had to be offered in soft-top form with folding hoods. Did that make them sports cars? Not in the sense of the Morgan, the Caterham Seven or the TVR, certainly. And eventually Rover (as British Leyland had become) realized that these obstinate specialists might have been right, and built the new MGF for the same kind of customer . . .

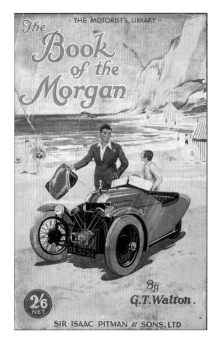

THE MOTORIST'S LIBRARY
The Book of the Morgan
By G.T. Walton.
2/6 NET
SIR ISAAC PITMAN & SONS, LTD

The Malvern-based Morgan company has remained faithful to its traditions ever since it was founded to make sporting three-wheelers (above). **By the 1960s its cars all had four wheels but retained 1930s looks and, for the most part, 1930s manufacturing methods.** *The Plus 4* (opposite, and previous spread) **was and still is the staple product, although there is also a V8-engined Plus 8. Morgan's only try at a more 'modern' design failed, but its customer order backlog remains one of the longest in the business.**

ROVER
2000 AND 3-LITRE MODELS

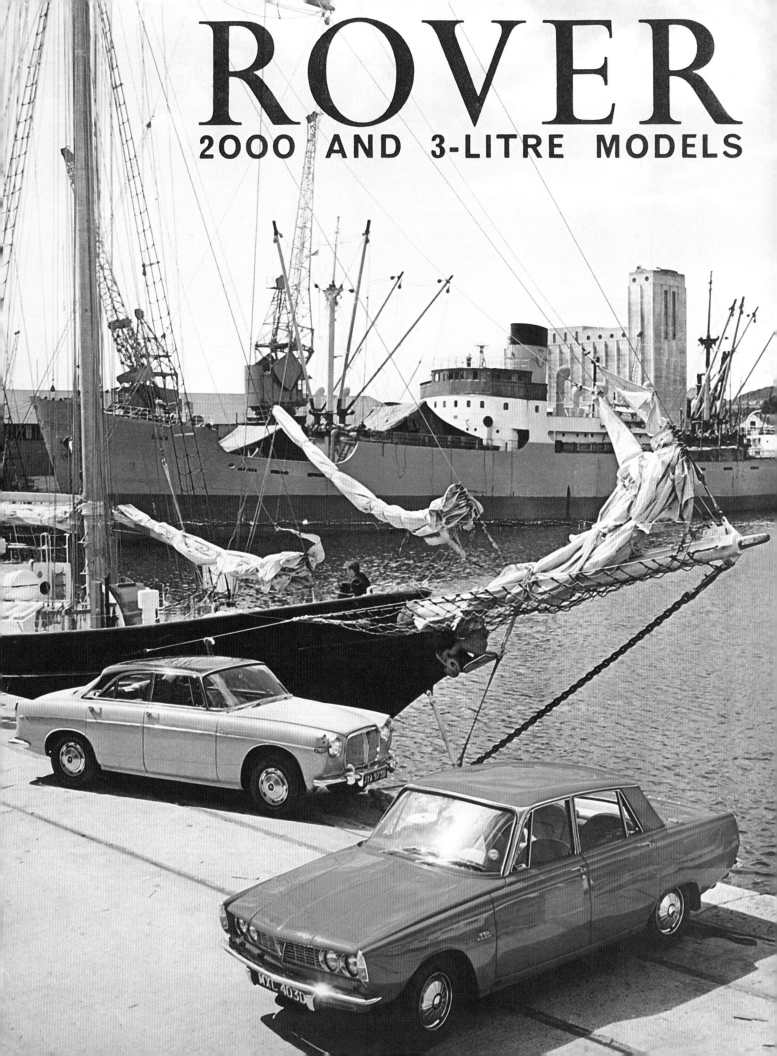

CHAPTER FOUR

EXECUTIVE CARS

*T*HE 1960S WAS THE DECADE in which the term 'executive car', in the sense of a car aimed at upper-level company managers, was coined. It was a peculiarly English-language phrase. Neither the French nor the Germans understood what we meant by it. Come to that, neither did the Americans. To make matters worse, it wasn't even accurate use of the language. As any British civil servant knows, within the service there are three career-structure 'ladders': low-level clerical, medium-grade executive, and high-flying administrative, the only one which leads to the very top. But who was going to call a new car model the Administrator, even for the sake of semantic accuracy? And so we moved through the 1960s talking more and more about 'executive' cars, which were class-consciously distinct from 'salesmen's cars', until Ford eventually took the hint and gave the name to one of its models (it also created high-trim versions like the Cortina 1600E and the Corsair 2000E, in which the E stood for . . . what else?).

There was more to all this than playing with words. The 1960s was also the decade in which the British, especially, changed the way they thought about cars for the better-off, and it happened because of a change in buying patterns. Traditionally, it had been the rich who bought big, fast, comfortable cars. The trouble was that in the aftermath of war, with very high income-tax levels (at one time, the top British rate was 98 per cent), there weren't enough rich people around to create a market of the size needed to keep several independent companies in business. Indeed, the market for such cars might have died almost completely – as it did in France, for example – had the British not invented a mechanism of substitution.

People didn't buy these large cars; companies did, for the members of their boards of management to travel in when on company business. Naturally there were other outlets, hire-car and taxi firms for example, and even funeral directors, but in

Rover's advertising in the 1960s often reflected the 'Viking ship' theme of the company badge. Here, the last of the old Rover line, the 3-litre Coupé with lowered roof and raked rear pillars, sits alongside the first of the new – the light, compact and efficient Rover 2000 which reshaped the way the British market thought about 'executive' cars.

Britain the size of the market was swollen by the way in which companies not only kept chauffeur-driven cars for their boards of directors, but increasingly issued smart cars for senior managers to drive themselves. The car was part of the salary, and a highly efficient part given the tax regulations of that time. So in Britain at least, through the 1950s, the market for what became the 'executive' car was sustained at a remarkably high level.

In fact, there were three levels. In 1960, if all you needed was a 'basic' big car, then four of the 'big five' British family car manufacturers offered a range-topping model. In fact, usually they offered two, one of them with few frills and aimed mainly at the taxi and hire-car trade, and the other (basically the same design) with more luxurious trim and equipment, sometimes with a little more power but always with a different name, aimed at the company buyer and the wealthy individual. Thus we had the Austin Westminster complemented by the Wolseley 6/99 (later the Wolseley 6/110), the Ford Zephyr and Zodiac, the Humber Hawk and the Super Snipe, and the Vauxhall Velox and Cresta. The mechanical hallmark of all these cars was a six-cylinder engine of around 3-litre capacity and 100hp, although the Humber Hawk made do with a four-cylinder engine, and Ford had the Zephyr 4 for anyone who wanted a big, impressive car but not the impressive performance to go with it. Considering the size of the domestic market – and very few of these cars were exported – the choice for the buyer was wide. The only large British manufacturer

The Austin Westminster was one of the 'old guard' of massive 3-litre cars with which the volume manufacturers topped their ranges. Above the Austin there was, of course, a Wolseley version: and above that, for a time, came the Vanden Plas Princess 4-litre R, with an extremely heavy but not very powerful six-cylinder Rolls-Royce engine replacing the BMC C-series power unit.

The Vauxhall Cresta was one of the Westminster's competitors. The PB-series car seen here (which many thought a better car than its successor the PC-series) came resplendent in two-tone paint. The American-style tail-fins were added part-way through this model's production life. The Velox was simply a Cresta built – or rather equipped and finished – down to a price.

not to compete at this level was Standard–Triumph, whose range stopped at the late-series 2-litre Vanguard. Cynically, you might have argued that this intense competition showed how much more profitable big cars were than little ones, or alternatively you could suggest that the major companies grimly hung on in the market because none of them wanted to be the first to admit defeat and be forced out of it.

If you wanted something rather more exclusive than a BMC or a Ford or a Vauxhall – or even a Humber, which was often seen as half a social class above the others – there were several of more elevated status from which to choose, though not as many as there had once been. A number of British 'prestige' marques – Alvis, Armstrong Siddeley and Lanchester among them – had re-entered the business after the war but lacked the financial strength to survive. Mostly they were absorbed into the larger companies. Alvis, builders of such elegant cars as the TC21/100 'Grey Lady', became part of Rover, ceased car production in the mid-1950s and turned entirely to the building of armoured vehicles. Armstrong Siddeley, its best-known late-series model probably being the 3.5-litre Sapphire, carried on until 1960 but then shut down to concentrate on building jet aero engines. Lanchester had actually been absorbed into Daimler as long ago as 1931, but distinct Lanchester models were built until 1954; they are probably admired more now than they were at the time. The era of the distinctive Riley models was already at an end: the handsome RMA and RME gave way first to the big Pathfinder, still with a unique body, and then to a sad series of badge-engineered BMC devices, including – horror of horrors – a version of the Mini with a Riley front grille!

These marques had all vanished by 1960 or were about to, but there were still up-market alternatives from which to choose. You might have the biggest Rover (the 3-litre), the biggest Jaguar (Mark IX) or a Daimler (Majestic or Majestic Major); or you could go to the very top (Rolls-Royce). At Rolls-Royce level, however, you were clearly no longer a mere executive, and the cars from that company rightly belong in Chapter Six.

In 1960 Rover remained independent, and the 3-litre was seen as distinctly handsome, even if today it appears a small-windowed heavyweight. Later in the decade it would be given a new lease of life with the removal of the hefty Rover six-cylinder, 3-litre engine, to be replaced by the light and powerful 3.5-litre V8 which Rover's Chairman had literally stumbled over while visiting the USA. There were lesser (but still very respectable) Rovers of course, but these were the cars for which the term 'Auntie' Rover had been coined. It implied, with fair accuracy, that they were heavy, safe, handsome but by no means beautiful, did everything rather slowly, and

were impeccably behaved. Few people in the 1960s had an inkling of the shock that Rover was about to deal the executive-car world.

If Rover was 'Auntie' then Jaguar was certainly a slightly raffish uncle, contriving to look rich without actually paying top-drawer prices, and with a strong interest in performance. As with Rover, you could choose the big Mark IX if you needed to make a weighty impression, or enjoy yourself rather more with the smaller, lighter and more nimble Mark 2, which was to gain such fame thirty years after it ended production, being driven around Oxford by Inspector Morse . . .

Above **The Rover 3-litre saloon makes an interesting comparison with the Coupé shown on page 98.** Opposite, top and bottom **The Humber Super Snipe was considered the most prestigious of the traditional large saloons. It was also sold in estate car form, though it is a matter of opinion whether a garish two-tone paint finish was really appropriate for a fairly dignified car.**

As for Daimler, 1960 saw the company finally encounter financial buffers, brought to a stop – or so it is often suggested – by the extravagance and wayward management of Sir Bernard Docker, whose wife, Lady Nora, was the moving spirit behind several outrageously opulent special-bodied cars which starred at early post-war Motor Shows. There was nothing mechanically different about these cars. Everything was down to styling, finish (gold plating, even) and trim and upholstery – in which exotic furs figured heavily. Nora Docker didn't care: she was bucking the trend of a dour, downtrodden Britain, with rationing still a part of life seven years after the end of the war. She was outrageous on purpose, but she helped bring Daimler to its knees. There was nothing much wrong with its cars, the Conquest (because, it is said, its original list price before tax was £1,066), the bigger Majestic and the stretched, and very imposing, Majestic Major which was famous among other things for being able to lap Silverstone as fast as almost any car on offer at the motoring journalists' annual production car Test Day. The Majestic, like its predecessors for many years, was a Royal favourite, and it survived for some time, but for the most part the Daimler name was steadily reduced through the 1960s to a series of badge-engineered Jaguars. The only exception was the massive Limousine, a kind of successor to the Majestic Major, designed specially for the chauffeur-driven market (and a favourite with the upper echelons of the funeral trade). This beast remained in small-scale production for many years, to the point where special exemptions were written into some safety legislation to allow it to continue.

The Daimler Limousine succeeded the well-loved Majestic Major but was essentially a Jaguar model, using the same engine as the XJ6. Hand-built in small numbers and consequently very expensive, it had a strong appeal for some users, not least the funeral trade. Sadly, although the car is large and impressive, the driving position is cramped and uncomfortable.

FOR EUROPEAN EXECUTIVES

Elsewhere in Europe, executive cars were distinctly thin on the ground, because nowhere else was there created a fleet-car market like that emerging in Britain. In France there was the Citroën DS, successor to the 'Big Six', which had taken the world by storm at its first showing and which had beyond doubt the most technically advanced chassis in the world. Sadly, it lacked a similarly advanced engine, but went well enough with the very ordinary four-cylinder one it had to please its customers. Renault had no serious DS rival, and Peugeot certainly didn't, at the time. During the 1970s, oddly enough, having absorbed Citroën complete with its DS successor, the CX, Peugeot finally launched its own 'prestige' car, the 604, but didn't do very well with it.

In the Germany of 1960 there was one true prestige manufacturer, in the shape of Mercedes. Ford of Germany and Opel made big cars of their own, the Taunus 26M and the Diplomat, but neither had anything like the cachet of the Mercedes. Even though the company's three-pointed star adorned the bonnets of most German taxis, there was a definite pecking-order on the *autobahn*. Everything else got out of the way of a Mercedes (if its driver had any sense), but the small Mercedes gave way to the bigger one. Foreign visitors were moved to admire the way in which German drivers seemed instantly able, with one glance in the mirror, to tell a mere Mercedes 190 from the mighty 300, when to the untutored eye the two did not look all that different unless they were parked side by side to reveal the contrast in actual size.

The Last Mile Is the Beginning for This Mercedes-Benz

In every new Mercedes-Benz, engine and transmission parts have already been bench tested at 200 miles per hour before assembly. Each bearing was X-rayed. Even the raw metals were analyzed by spectroscope.
Now, on a misty evening, this Mercedes-Benz faces its traditional final trial — a test engineer will take it over a specially constructed track. He will summon the full capacity of its new aluminum fuel-injection engine. He will back it, try to stall it, listen with trained ears. Does it spurt ahead when called upon? Does it idle so he can hear the whisper of its exhaust only by stepping out of the automobile?
Not until the Engineering Department has officially approved this motorcar will it be shipped here, to your Mercedes-Benz dealer.
You too should try this great Mercedes-Benz at your dealer's. This week. And ask him how you can save the cost of a vacation in Europe — by taking delivery there.

Mercedes-Benz Sales, Inc. (A Subsidiary of Studebaker Corporation) South Bend, Indiana

The sign of the three-pointed star: Mercedes recovered quickly after the war and by the 1960s were building cars like this 300. Prestige buyers seemed not to care that the lesser Mercedes models had become the standard taxi, not only of Germany but many other cities around the world. As the advertisement suggests, Mercedes was one of the earliest manufacturers to conduct serious research into crash-safety.

Given the rapidly increasing size and wealth of the German market, others eyed it greedily. It did them little good, unless they were German too. The rise of BMW, especially in the latter years of the 1960s when the engineers in Munich began to extend the 'new class' principles to bigger cars, had much to do with the relief of better-off German buyers that at last they could afford to be different without compromising their devotion to the highest engineering standards. Later on, though not to any extent during the 1960s, Volkswagen would attempt to raise Audi into contention with Mercedes and BMW, though not with complete success.

The Italian market for large, luxury cars should have been too small to support even one national manufacturer. However, even in a country with only one car for every twenty-five people, as in 1959, Italy had a notable number of landowners and industrialists, not to mention the upper levels of the church hierarchy, and such people expected to travel in a certain style. The manufacturer who most often obliged was Lancia, whose big, beautifully made and expensive Flaminia was often cheerfully referred to as 'the

Above **The Lancia Flaminia, as a four-door saloon or more rarely the two-door Coupé seen here, was Italy's best-known executive car of the 1960s – but was dropped when Fiat took over the company.**

Below **The Lincoln was (and is) a leading challenger for the affections of American buyers looking for a touch of class – huge and soft like all of its kind, but surprisingly tough and reliable too.**

Vatican taxi'. The giant Fiat was not directly involved in this market, although through the 1960s its top-range cars became larger until at the very end of the decade, it launched the 3-litre 130, which was well engineered but which most people thought looked too much like an over-ornate Italian interpretation of the Mercedes saloon theme (although an exquisite large two-door coupé built on the same chassis by Pininfarina was universally admired). Alfa Romeo offered a bigger car, the 2600, but most knowledge-able onlookers said it only went to show that while Alfa built very pleasant and capable medium-sized cars (the Giulietta and Giulia range) its big ones were nothing like so nice.

These three major manufacturers apart, post-war Italy also saw the coming into existence of a number of companies who took advantage of the country's flair for engineering and for skilled manual metal-shaping. Hydraulic presses might be the only way of stamping out body panels in large numbers, but such presses were expensive. If you needed to build only a thousand or so bodies in a year, you could fill a shop with men who would take sheets of (usually) aluminium, and who would manoeuvre them between rollers, tweak and snip and fold them to produce panels which, when attached to a suitable frame, would form car bodies that were both light and beautiful. This unique way of working, which could really only have happened in Italy, permitted the resurgence of Maserati, and the birth of Ferrari, and eventually during the 1960s gave rise to Lamborghini; but the progress and products of such companies are really for Chapter Six.

AMERICA AND JAPAN

The idea of an executive car was, and is, entirely strange to Americans. Whatever kind of class structure exists in the USA, it has never extended to determining what kind of car people buy or drive, in the way it certainly does in the UK. If a successful American plumber or carpenter wants to buy a big Cadillac, that is his business, while his British counterpart buying a Rolls-Royce would probably be accused of putting on airs, both by his customers and by his colleagues in the trade. It was even more so during the 1960s.

As a result, the Americans went on building cars which simply gave people the choice: the more they wanted to spend, the more car they got. The only

Europeans usually think of the Cadillac as the 'top' American car – and usually think in terms of models like this 1960s Fleetwood. At the time, many well-heeled American buyers probably thought it the epitome of restrained elegance. From the perspective of the 1990s, it looks like a medium-sized car trapped inside a large steel box and in urgent need of escape. Cadillacs of this era had some of the largest engines ever seen in mass-produced cars: V8s of up to 8.2 litres.

way you could aspire to making a more 'personal statement' than the top Chrysler, Lincoln (Ford) or Cadillac was to buy an extremely expensive import or to have a car specially modified in some way. But all that did was to show other people you were richer – not necessarily that you were in some way superior, which was what the British 'executive car' syndrome was all about.

Likewise, though for different reasons, Japan has never had executive cars. What it did develop, fairly quickly, was a market for large chauffeur-driven cars for senior company managers. The reason for this was that Japan had come so late to the concept of the private car that many Japanese of a certain age had never learned to drive – and were now perhaps afraid to try, for fear of losing face through failure. In 1960 it was much easier for them, if they were beginning to earn money from their early involvement in a rapidly expanding business, to buy not only a large and comfortable car, a Toyota Century or a Nissan President, but the services of a smart young man to drive it for them. It is a custom that continues to this day – although the sons of those early non-drivers keep it now as a tradition, and have their own expensive imported cars tucked away for their private driving pleasure!

EXECUTIVE EVOLUTION

The main trend of development during the 1960s was that people became fed up with the conventional large, 3-litre executive car, deciding that size need not be directly related to prestige or executive status. It was an evolution that was encouraged by the appearance of one or two remarkable new cars, and by the economics of the industry itself.

So far as the conventional large executive cars were concerned, the field was slimmed early in the 1960s by the disappearance of the big Humbers. They weren't replaced: Rootes Group simply withdrew from the executive market, nibbling at its lower edges with the plushest of its mid-range cars, the Humber Sceptre, which was no more than a badge-engineered Hillman Super Minx. The reason, quite simply, was that the company couldn't afford the cost of developing a 'big Humber' replacement at a time when it was already struggling to contain the development cost of the new small Imp (which appeared in 1963) and the new Hillman Hunter, due to replace the existing Minx/Gazelle series later in the 1960s. Canny minds within the Rootes Group may also have foreseen that the Humber's market was about to fall on hard times.

There were no such doubts at BMC, where as a strange offshoot of the plan to create a range of 'Issigonis' products, the Austin Westminster and Wolseley 6/110 gave way in 1967 to the Austin 3-litre. This was a hideously 'stretched' adaptation of the front-driven 1800 with the same centre section, but a longer bonnet and boot. It needed the longer bonnet to accommodate a lengthwise 3-litre six-cylinder engine – lengthwise because the 3-litre reverted to rear wheel drive. The ride comfort should have been good, because the car used a complicated, further developed version of the Hydragas system from the 1800. In the event, however, the Austin 3-litre failed miserably. It wasn't just that the market for which it had been designed was shrinking. Too many people rightly asked why a car with less cabin space than the 1800 (less, because of the transmission tunnel passing through it) and hardly any more performance, should cost half as much again and use twice as much petrol. If there were any plans for a Wolseley version of the 3-litre, they were shelved in the light of this failure and also, no doubt, because BMC was close to the final creation of British Leyland, which would include Rover.

The 1960s also saw Ford commit one of its rare product planning blunders with its introduction of the Mark 4 series Zephyr and Zodiac (with, at one point, a highly specified top version actually christened the Executive). The Mark 4 was a very 'American' car in many ways, with an extremely long nose and a flat-topped bonnet – so much so that wags began calling it the 'aircraft carrier' – and a short tail. To make enough space for luggage in the back, the spare wheel was carried at the front of the long nose, behind the radiator grille. Further amusement was caused when it was noticed that the word 'Ford' did not, to begin with, appear anywhere on the car, as though the company had somehow grown ashamed of itself. Much less amusing was the car's handling, which was badly affected by an extremely odd (and never repeated) independent rear suspension arrangement, compounded by a disastrous choice of tyre equipment. Even without this problem, the Mark 4 range would probably never have made it, even with Rootes Group dropping out of the market and BMC in decline. In the event, it soldiered on unloved until Ford was able to replace it with the first Granada, but by then it had given people yet another reason to dislike the idea of the large executive car from a volume manufacturer.

Vauxhall did very little to help the cause either. True, the company was forced to accept that the series PB Cresta, one of the few cars arguably inferior in most respects to the one it replaced, was a disastrous evocation of soft, 'wallowy' American chassis design ill-suited to British and European conditions. Vauxhall tried to make amends with the PC series which appeared in 1966. It was an improvement, and it was followed by a better equipped up-market version called the Viscount, a clear answer to Ford's Executive; but in the end it wasn't good enough, and from the early 1970s Vauxhall's shrinking band of big-car customers were given Opel designs.

THE EXECUTIVE

In the distinguished world of the Executive the luxury of automatic transmission, power steering and a steel sliding sun roof can be taken for granted. And the very advanced specification includes a smooth 3-litre V6 engine, four wheel independent suspension and power assisted disc brakes on all four wheels.
Inside this fine car the appointments are superb. The facia is burr walnut, the upholstery is crushed hide or broadcloth to choice. The fitted radio has twin speakers, the individually reclining front seats have neat inertia reel seat belts. The whole interior is temperature-controlled by the unique *Aeroflow* heating and ventilation system. Even the boot is close carpeted. Throughout the Executive you will find features which on other cars are optional extras. These are just part of the distinguished world of the Executive which awaits you at the showroom of your local Ford Dealer.

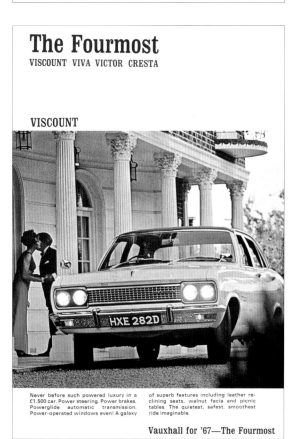

The Fourmost
VISCOUNT · VIVA · VICTOR · CRESTA

VISCOUNT

Never before such powered luxury in a £1,500 car. Power steering. Power brakes. Powerglide automatic transmission. Power-operated windows even! A galaxy of superb features including leather reclining seats, walnut facia and picnic tables. The quietest, safest, smoothest ride imaginable.

Vauxhall for '67—The Fourmost

THE ROVER–TRIUMPH CHALLENGE

The development that caused all the trouble for the conventional 'big' executive cars was a two-pronged attack from Triumph and Rover. Both companies brought out cars which they called simply 2000, within months of each other in 1963. Triumph did theirs as a replacement for the Standard Vanguard; Rover set out to create a modern replacement for its 'Auntie' series. In many ways, the thinking that went into the two models ran remarkably parallel (and it was parallel; security on both projects was kept extremely tight). The thinking was this: do 'executives' really want their cars to be large? Suppose we make the car large enough to provide four comfortable seats, but subject to that need, keep it as small as possible and instead spend the money we thus save on technical features to improve comfort and performance, and on a suitably high standard of equipment? Suppose, in fact, that for the same price we offer our customers a car with 'executive' comfort, performance and specification, but nimbler and more economical because it is smaller and lighter than the 3-litre monsters they are used to? Can we create a medium-sized car with true 'executive' status?

Both teams decided that it was possible. There were differences of philosophy in their interpretations, but the overall concept was clear. The Triumph 2000 had a six-cylinder engine, the Rover 2000 had a new four-cylinder, overhead camshaft unit. The Triumph used semi-trailing independent rear suspension, the Rover a complicated variation of the de Dion system. The Triumph had a bench back seat, while the Rover back seat was divided into two quite distinct places, accepting that a third,

The Triumph 2000, here with Monaco harbour in the background, was the Rover 2000's deadly rival. Its biggest advantage in the sales battle, apart from a lower price, was its smooth six-cylinder engine, while Rover used a four-cylinder. In many respects, though, the two cars were astonishingly similar – a case of two product-planning teams thinking in parallel.

The Rover 2000, seen here in something close to its original form, had the edge over the Triumph in sheer prestige. Among its achievements, it managed to convince up-market British buyers that cars could impress through purity of line and quality of finish, without needing masses of chrome trim. At one time, it was foreseen that the squared-off bonnet might one day cover a gas turbine engine, in which Rover was long interested; but that was just a dream.

squeezed-in rear passenger would be less comfortable. Most interestingly, Triumph kept its 2000 launch price just below £1,000, the psychological break-point at which the cheapest versions of the 'big' cars were also priced, while Rover allowed itself to go some way beyond.

Between them, the two new cars were a staggering success. Despite its higher price, the Rover sold better; but their main impact was in winning thousands of orders from people who would previously have bought 'big' cars almost without thinking. The Rover in particular become *the* smart car in which to arrive, and demand exceeded supply for some time. Indeed, when Rover brought out a more powerful 2000TC (Twin Carburettor) version, initial production was for export only, harking back fifteen years to the time when almost all British car production had been on that basis. Triumph countered with an estate version of its 2000 – there never was any 'official' Rover 2000 estate, although several coachbuilders produced prototypes of their own – and a more powerful 2.5PI, one of the first British production cars to offer fuel injection instead of carburettors. Sadly, the Lucas system used by Triumph was plagued with problems and eventually this more powerful version become the 2500TC with carburettors.

Rover had no easy way of making its four-cylinder engine more powerful, but it found it could fit the 3.5-litre V8 into the 2000, helped by the fact that the car's unusual front suspension had originally been designed to leave a clear 'cube' of space for a possible gas turbine engine (from 1949, Rover had demonstrated a series of gas-turbine-powered prototypes). The Rover 3500 – as distinct from the 'big' 3.5-litre which had been the first user of that engine – was by no means as much of a beast as some might have predicted.

Eventually, both the Rover and the Triumph gave way during the 1970s to a single British Leyland replacement design, the Rover 3500 or SD1. Long before that, however, the message had come through loud and clear to the volume manufacturers whose largest cars had been so comprehensively usurped by the newcomers. BMC and its successors had no worries since they would embrace Rover and Triumph, but Ford and Vauxhall gave thought to the situation and responded as best they could. What it amounted to was that they must fight the Rover and Triumph 2000s with the plushest possible versions of their own medium-sized cars.

For Vauxhall, that meant adapting the Victor, which in the late 1960s metamorphosed from the unloved FC series to the considerably larger FD. This new car appeared complete with a new 2-litre engine and, with suitable equipment and trim, might have provided a viable competitor in the new market. It failed to make an impact, partly because the car had its faults but also because Vauxhall simply wasn't the same thing as Rover and Triumph. Snobbishness, for those who chose to see it that way, still reigned. Vauxhall refused to give up and tried shoehorning the big and heavy six-cylinder engine from the Cresta into the Victor, creating a faster, but nose-heavy version which it called the Ventora; it failed to make its mark.

Then as now, the Italian Riviera was a favourite background for car publicity photographs. This is the 'Executive' version of the Ford Zodiac Mark III, the car which was replaced by the slab-sided, long-bonneted Mark 4. This Zodiac, and its lesser cousin the Zephyr, sold strongly in the traditional executive car market until values shifted to smaller cars and more restrained styling.

Ford took the challenge more seriously. After all, during the mid-1960s it had an intermediate model, the Corsair, which fitted into the range between the Cortina and the Zephyr/Zodiac. It had flopped initially, but enjoyed something of a revival when fitted with a 2-litre engine, much improved trim and equipment, and a minor master-stroke of styling: a stuck-on fabric roof reminiscent of the old Riley RME. The new version was designated 2000E, making it clear that the Corsair in this form was intended to appeal to the Rover–Triumph market. Even if it didn't completely fulfil these aspirations, it began a fashion of its own and before long, there was also a fabric-roofed 1600E version of the Cortina Mark 2, launched in 1966. And when the significantly larger Cortina Mark 3 was launched in 1970, that offered a 2000E version from the outset. They may not have been great cars, but they helped to wean away the market from the idea that it was the car model that mattered: now, a medium-sized model could span a range of versions from 'entry level' to 'aspiring executive', and that in turn would shape the product planning of subsequent decades.

HIGHER UP THE SCALE

While this battle was being waged between the new generation of compact executive cars and the battleships of an earlier generation, Jaguar continued on its independent way with very little genuine competition at its chosen market level. If you wanted to spend something between £2,000 and £3,000 on a new car in the early 1960s, you either bought Jaguar, or you tried a Mercedes, or if you were brave you risked any of a number of more or less exotic imports, some of which enjoyed far too little in the way of spare parts and service backing.

So far as its saloon car range was concerned, Jaguar eased its way into the 1960s with the Mark X, its first big car to have independent rear suspension. The impact of the Mark X's launch was rather lost amid the understandable fuss surrounding the launch of the E-type, but the car sold well enough – at its value-for-money price of under £2,500 at launch – to plug most of the gap between the new Rover and Triumph 2000s and the Rolls-Royce range. By now its only possible British rival was the 'big' Rover 3/3.5-litre, which was neither as roomy nor as fast, but which many people saw as more dignified (it remained the standard government ministerial transport for many years).

Throughout the 1960s Jaguar updated the Mark X with a 4.2-litre engine and even introduced a new 'in-between' S-type, a sort of Mark 2 but with independent rear suspension; but in 1968 the company managed to astonish the world for the second time in a decade with the all-new XJ6 which replaced both the Mark X and the S-type, and which was to become its staple product, through various stages of evolution, for almost two decades (until the launch of the XJ40, in 1986).

What made the XJ6 so good? Even those who designed it were pushed to explain exactly how they had done it, but the word was refinement. True, the car had all the performance one would have expected with a 4.2-litre engine, and its manoeuvrabil-

In 1968 Jaguar took the motoring world by storm for a second time that decade, with the launch of the XJ6. The last model whose styling was personally overseen by Jaguar's founder Sir William Lyons, it set new standards for executive saloon handling, roadholding and sheer refinement. The only possible complaint was that the back seat wasn't quite roomy enough; Jaguar answered that by offering a long wheelbase version.

ity and cornering powers were a considerable step forward from the Mark X in particular. However, it was its quietness and smoothness that marked it out as an exceptional achievement. The engine whispered, and very little noise or vibration came through to the cabin from the road surface. For several years, the motor industry had generally taken the Peugeot 404 as the guiding standard where refinement was concerned, but the Jaguar XJ6 effectively replaced it. From then on, it was the target at which everyone else aimed when it came to the 'magic carpet' aspects of car design and development. Like everyone else in the British motor industry, Jaguar was destined for some hard times through the 1970s but at least the XJ6 provided it with a winner, a firm foundation. Eventually the car would be stretched into a long wheelbase version, for those who complained that the back seat was a little on the tight side; and very soon, a magnificent V12 engine would appear, still further to enhance the refinement of the car's most expensive versions. Almost the only thing to spoil the reputation of the XJ6 was the offer of a smaller capacity, 'tax special' 2.8-litre engine, aimed mainly at European export markets. It soon emerged that in Europe, anyone who could afford an XJ6 could afford – and wanted – the 4.2-litre engine. The biggest takers for the 2.8-litre were British buyers who thought it would be more economical. It wasn't, and the engine proved less reliable into the bargain, but that should never detract from the overall achievement which the car represented.

HOW IT ENDED – AND WHERE WE HAVE COME

Today, we are all quite used to 'executives' driving around in well-equipped Ford Mondeos and Vauxhall Vectras, which shows both how far the market shifted and how the volume manufacturers eventually got to work in the most effective way. These, sadly, are the sons of the Rover and Triumph 2000s. The story of the company that absorbed both of those names is worth a book in itself. To say the least, it is no longer a major player. Yet there are plenty of competitors in 1999's executive market. Some of them are imports, and some come from British factories with names that would have astonished anyone from 1960 who could see them now: Honda, Nissan, Peugeot, Toyota. The British fleet-car market has become a social hierarchy in its own right, and everyone seems to know the value and the implied prestige of every model on the market. So marketing in its turn has become a matter of trying to 'position' new and existing models. Simply creating a good car, unfortunately, is no longer enough . . .

LMV 644C

CHAPTER FIVE

ECONOMY CARS

℥ROM TIME TO TIME, there is a surge of interest in cars that are as economical as possible. The interest usually arises when, for political reasons, fuel suddenly becomes more expensive or supplies threaten to run short. As it happens, there was one such event – the Suez crisis – shortly before the 1960s began, and another – the first Middle East war and the threat of an oil supply embargo by the then-powerful OPEC – shortly after it finished. Consequently, the 1960s began with everybody, in the UK and Europe at least, desperately interested in economy, and then saw a steady drift of that interest towards performance and comfort, as fuel prices stabilized and people generally became better off. Then, through the 1970s, the cycle was played out once again, to be repeated once more in the early 1980s.

There is only one formula for an economy car which really works, and that is to make the vehicle itself as small and light as possible. The dream of a normal-sized car with a 'miracle' engine yielding 100mpg is just that – a dream; at least, it's a dream unless you have available the kind of technology that is only now being developed and which will be seen in the cars of 2005 or thereabouts.

The most obvious recipe for an economy car in the mid-1950s was therefore to take two seats, create the lightest possible body tightly around them, and then install a tiny single-cylinder or two-cylinder engine, probably beneath and behind the seats, to provide the minimum acceptable performance. This was the theory behind the rash of bubble cars that emerged during the 1950s and gained a brief but real popularity in the aftermath of the Suez crisis. They didn't last long, for all manner of reasons. One was that 'minimum acceptable performance' meant one thing when it looked as though petrol was going to be rationed as well as expensive, and something else when it became clear things were going to get better. Another was that generally speaking, people don't like two-seater cars, unless they are sports cars. Although the

A truly British bubble-car, the Peel Trident: tiny engine, tiny plastic body with cramped seating for two, minimal performance, poor handling, and crash safety behaviour which was, fortunately, never called into question. But it would return 100mpg, and in any case, are we entitled to judge vehicles like this by conventional car standards? As long as they run on the same roads, sadly, we probably are.

average car in the UK actually carries 1.18 people – in other words, most of them contain only the driver – buyers still want four seats, so that they can carry the whole family, or a couple of colleagues or friends, when the occasion demands.

There had been an earlier 'economy car' era, in the 1920s, just after the First World War. The idea then was to make a car which was simple and therefore cheap enough to reach a mass market. Those cars were called 'cyclecars' for the simple reason that they mostly ran on four heavyweight bicycle wheels: glorified soap-boxes with tiny engines. Some of these devices were ingenious and worked quite well within their obvious limitations, while others were disastrous. Invariably, however, the manufacturing companies set up to make them did their sums all wrong. They were never able to make the cyclecars as cheap as they had predicted, and because they missed out on price, they missed out on the market. Then, just when they were teetering on the brink anyway, the original Austin Seven came along and cut away the edge of their cliff. For a few pounds more, buyers could have a 'proper' car by the standards of the time – and that was the option they chose. It was a lesson of history from which, thirty years later, the bubble car manufacturers signally failed to learn.

At the root of their failure is the fact that once you have a compact two-seat car, you don't need to extend it by very much – perhaps by a foot – to provide two extra seats in the back, even though they may be small ones, without making the car very much heavier. This was something of which the established car manufacturers were well aware, having done all their sums many years before. This in turn explains why the bubble cars came mostly from companies who were new to the business. Some of them were former aircraft companies: among the popular badges seen on the bubble cars of the 1950s were Heinkel and Messerschmitt, leading to the joke that we only needed

Above *The bubble car was in vogue, as 'Town Travel in the Space Age', long enough to attract the attention of satirical motoring cartoonist Red Daniells, who drew this typically trendy owner.*

Right *The remarkable Messerschmitt carried its two occupants in tandem. While not very sociable, the layout reduced width and frontal area, so improving economy, and made for better handling. The 500cc Messerschmitt Tiger, with twin rear wheels, was astonishingly fast too.*

Junkers, Dornier and Focke-Wulf to make a full set. The Heinkel was actually built under licence in Britain, by the Trojan company. Other companies were formed by optimists who thought they had a better design of bubble car than anyone else, and that the bubble car was the transport of the future.

Some of the smaller car manufacturers, especially in Germany, *were* drawn to the bubble concept. They suffered for it when the bubble market burst. The Goggomobil, for example, came from Hans Glas, otherwise a maker of neat medium-sized saloons and sports coupés, but doomed to be absorbed into BMW. The Lloyd – a German product despite its name – was produced by a subsidiary of Borgward, the respected maker of the Isabella and other medium-sized cars. At one time the two-cylinder, 300cc Lloyd was the fourth best-selling car in Germany, ahead of Ford of Germany and DKW for example, moving out of the showrooms at a rate of a thousand a week during 1955; but Borgward was not far from being driven out of the car business altogether.

But in any case, why 'bubble car'? It was simply because with a minimum body drawn around two people seated side by side tending to be as wide as it is long, and with the corners being rounded-off, the similarity becomes obvious. In fact many of the 'bubbles', including the Heinkel and the BMW-Isetta, were shaped like fat teardrops, with two small wheels at the front and a single wheel (or two close-coupled wheels) at the rear, in close association with the tiny engine. It was not an arrangement which lent itself to brilliant stability and handling, so it is perhaps fortunate that bubble car performance was fairly limited. There was also the problem of access, which was often solved by having the entire front of the car hinge open, complete with universal-jointed steering column. There were all manner of jokes at the time about not parking nose-on to a wall (the more so since some designs used adapted motor cycle gearboxes without a reverse gear), and more seriously there was the question of how you got out if you were unlucky enough to run into something.

Not all the cars in the class conformed to the same formula, though: the Messerschmitt seated its two occupants in tandem beneath a side-hinged canopy, and was consequently remarkably narrow. The Messerschmitt layout also overcame the problem that in a very small, light car with side-by-side seats, the offset weight of the driver can make a real

Above *Jackie Collins, her first novel still years away, does her best to make the BMW 600 look attractive. The shock effect of the outfit may have helped divert attention from the look of the car.*

Below *You parked the BMW Isetta nose-on to the kerb and opened the front door to get out. Such imaginative features, and outstanding economy, were not enough to keep sales going once buyers were no longer worried where their next gallon was coming from.*

119

difference to the handling. Most of the side-by-side 'bubbles', with only the driver aboard, would corner noticeably better in one direction than the other. Normally, the Messerschmitt had a single wheel at the back and a 200cc engine, but the Tiger was a version with twin rear wheels and 500cc power unit, practically a performance car by bubble standards and well thought of in its brief day.

There were bubbles that seated four. The Zundapp Janus (Zundapp was normally a motor cycle maker) was virtually symmetrical,

Above **Renault's first serious contribution to the economy-car stakes was the 4CV or 750. Despite its conventional appearance, this car too was rear-engined.**

with its engine in the middle, sandwiched between two forward-facing seats at the front and two rear-facing ones behind, and a big outward-hinged door at each end. One of the best-known bubble cars was the Isetta, an Italian design from the Iso company – also responsible for two 'supercars', the Grifo and the Rivolta. The Isetta (which is Italian for 'little Iso') proved popular in Italy in the mid-1950s, even to the extent that a special class was created for them in the famous Mille Miglia road race. Further success came to the little bubble car when it was taken up by BMW as a way of filling its factories and keeping the cash flowing while it sorted out its parlous financial position. BMW prudently threw away the smoky Italian two-stroke engine and substituted one of its own 250cc four-stroke motor-cycle engines before offering it to German buyers. As produced by BMW, the Isetta had 12hp to propel it to a claimed maximum speed of 53mph; the fuel tank held 3½ gallons (13 litres) and would take it 200 gently driven miles. Normally the Isetta had twin close-coupled wheels at the back, but for the British market BMW did a version with just one rear wheel, to take advantage of the cheaper three-wheeler road tax. British-market Isettas were sold by AFN, a company much better known as the British Porsche concession-

Opposite **Fiat created an early 'people carrier' with the 600 Multipla. The whole of this extended family – and the picnic – really did fit into this astonishing little machine, derived from the rear-engined 600 saloon.**

Left **The Citroën 2CV was perhaps the most celebrated 'economy special' of all. Millions were built from the late 1940s to the late 1980s. With front-mounted flat-twin engine and long-travel suspension, the 2CV really could be driven across a ploughed field.**

aire of long standing! There was also a plan to make the car in Britain under licence, but the entire bubble market collapsed before preparations could be completed.

Although BMW built and sold over 160,000 Isettas, the company became worried when sales began to fall away and in 1957 it produced a 'super bubble', the BMW 600, whose lengthened body retained the single nose-door but also provided two small rear side doors giving access to a cramped rear bench seat. The engine became a flat-twin, again borrowed from a BMW motor cycle, and delivered almost 20hp, enough for a maximum speed of around 60mph. But the 600 did not win favour and BMW moved on very quickly to the 700, which used a very similar mechanical layout but was outwardly a 'proper' car with styling by the Italian Michelotti. The BMW 700 was one of a clutch of very small and economical cars that were most definitely not bubbles. These included the extremely neat little rear-engined NSU Prinz 4, a basic design good enough to be 'stretched' into the Prinz 1000 and eventually the 1200, a roomy rival for the VW Beetle and according to many road testers of the time, a nicer car to drive. There was also the DKW Junior, front-driven and enjoying a solid engineering pedigree. All these cars helped to do away with the bubbles, several years before NSU became part of the Volkswagen group, and DKW, after being turned into Audi, did likewise.

For the most part, the established car manufacturers stoutly resisted the temptation to travel the bubble-car road. In Europe, the French already had their minimalist four-seaters, the Citroën 2CV and the Renault 4CV, and saw all too well that to build anything smaller would merely poach sales from these models. In other words, the payoff for spending quite a lot on the development of a new ultra-small model would inevitably be slimmer margins and lower profits. Far better to let some upstart company try their luck and go to the wall! In its earliest form the Citroën 2CV in particular had little more power than some of the bubbles – with a flat-twin engine of 425cc and 12hp (the Renault 4CV had a four-cylinder, 748cc engine producing a princely 19hp!). The appeal of the Citroën, however, lay in the roominess of its body, even if it did appear to be made from corrugated iron, and in the amazing comfort provided by its uniquely absorbent suspension – despite the fact that this same softness allowed the car to roll most alarmingly when cornered.

Fiat's Nuova 500, successor to the pre-war Topolino, again went the rear-engined route. It was one of the most successful ultra-small economy cars, because it was a 'real car' on a small scale rather than a crude and simple 'bubble'. This 500 was built in its millions and remained in production for many years, until finally replaced by the Fiat 126 which continued the company tradition.

In Italy, Fiat was already building cars which, in some ways, were bubbles – except that they were cars with a wheel at each corner, four-cylinder engines, and a pedigree. The Fiat 600, launched in 1955, had become as much of an Italian staple as its famous predecessor the 500, the 'Topolino'. It quickly became the biggest-selling car in Italy, and with four only slightly grudging seats and a top speed of over 60mph, it made a nonsense

If you are going to be minimal, be truly minimal: this is the Peel P50, made by the same company that designed the Trident. A Cyclops-eyed single-seater with three tiny wheels, the P50 exemplifies the problems which still face economy-car innovators. Who is going to buy a vehicle with this limited level of performance and such poor refinement? Especially, who is going to buy it if it costs half as much as a decent four-seat car? Except in times of emergency, you need more selling points than pure economy.

of most of the bubble cars. Nor was that the end of the matter, because Fiat quickly followed up with a Nuova 500, in effect a scaled-down 600, with a two-cylinder engine but otherwise following the same formula. Fiat's efforts even extended to a six-seater 600 Multipla – a 'multi-purpose people-mover' a quarter of a century before the idea was reinvented – and a neat little Giardiniera estate version of the new 500. These were tricks that the bubble car fraternity simply couldn't match.

THE BRITISH BUBBLE SCENE

In the UK, as elsewhere, the bubble car was something of a craze for a few short years during the 1950s. A handful of tiny specialist companies tried to make their own versions of the concept work: among them Peel in the Isle of Man, the Frisky, and the BSA Ladybird – this last from a company at the very heart of British engineering, and which should surely have known better, even though the Ladybird was decently engineered and one of the better vehicles of its type.

An attempt, however misguided, at applying modern car styling to the ultra-economy car – in this case the British-made Frisky. At least, if you are going to have only three wheels, this is the way round to have them: two in front, one at the lightly laden rear. It would have helped, however, if among other details the doors had been front rather than rear-hinged. In any case, by the time the Frisky was launched, the bubble-car boom had burst.

The UK tax regime created some odd situations. For example, as related in Chapter Three, purchase tax could be avoided by buying cars in kit form and assembling them in one's own workshop, while vehicles with only three wheels were classified as being motor-cycle and sidecar combinations and paid a lower rate of annual road tax (and if reverse gear was blanked off, you were allowed to drive them on a motor-bike driver's licence, without taking the car driving test). The long-established car enthusiast magazines of the day, *The Motor* and *The Autocar*, took a leaf from the tax-man's book and decided that three-wheelers were not proper cars and they would not normally mention them. But *The Autocar* did run a road test of a BMW Isetta during 1955 (mean maximum speed 50.8mph, 0–40mph in 22.7 seconds, overall fuel consumption 61mpg for 158 miles); one suspects a story behind this glaring exception to the rule, possibly associated with the subsequent publication of 'road impressions' of a Porsche 356 loaned by the same importer, followed by a full road test of a similar car on the Continent! The Isetta road test concluded that 'Selling at a total price in this country comparable with that of the least expensive conventional cars (£292 plus £123 purchase tax), and providing a high degree of economy, this BMW may well find a niche in the British market. There are no innovations incorporated in the design or construction that are not included for practical reasons; thus although the car is unusual it is honest.' Experts in 1950s 'road-test-speak' will rightly interpret this to mean 'anyone would be mad to buy this weird little device at this price'. Such was the appeal of the 61mpg, however, that several thousand people did.

Meanwhile, a number of ingenious minds embraced the twin tax advantages of 'kit' three-wheelers and decided there was a fortune to be made selling cars that would be cheap both to buy and to tax, leaving customers to assemble their tiny economy devices in their own garages. This seems now to be a recipe for disaster: at least the buyers of kit-built sports cars would be enthusiasts with some chance of mechanical knowledge and understanding, but people buying little economy run-abouts were another matter. In the absence of anything to stop them, though, some entrepreneurs obviously felt the British public would find it hard to resist the idea of doing down the tax-man twice in one go.

By no means all the lightweight British kit cars were bubbles, even if they were three-wheelers. The Biggleswade-based Berkeley company, its products designed by Laurie Bond who was also the originator of the Bond Minicar, made neat, low-slung little cars with a distinctly 'sports' look to them. Bond was one of the pioneers of glass-reinforced plastic (grp) construction, making his cars as a few large mouldings stiffened with riveted aluminium beams. Even with a very small engine, the very light weight of such a body promised good performance, and you could almost hear the sigh of relief from the editorial staffs of the motoring magazines when Berkeley produced a model with two rear wheels instead of just one, and they were allowed to talk about it.

The Berkeley looked like a shrunken version of a 'proper' sports car, its 12in wheels providing exactly the right proportions. Under its glass-reinforced plastic bonnet, the arrangement was distinctly unusual, with a two-stroke engine installed trans-

A sporting three-wheeler rather in the original Morgan tradition but with 1960s styling and plastic body, the front-driven, motorcycle-engined Berkeley gained a strong following during its short period of production. Eventually the three-wheelers were joined, then supplanted, by versions with four wheels. In the end, however, Berkeley was unable to survive the market's loss of interest in fuel economy.

versely, a chain drive to a four-speed gearbox, and a second chain drive to the differential, driving the front wheels.

By the standards of its day the little Berkeley was no slouch. In four-wheeled form it began life with a two-cylinder engine, but by the time *The Autocar* tested one in 1958, it had acquired a three-cylinder engine of 492cc and a claimed 30hp. Thus powered, it returned a mean maximum speed of 80mph, 0–60mph acceleration of 21.8 seconds, but had a rather disastrous fuel consumption, given its low weight and small size, of 33.1mpg – so you would have had to refill its 5-gallon tank every 150 miles to be on the safe side! One has the impression that if Berkeley had been able to graduate to something bigger and better, it might have become one of the long-lived 'minnows' of the British industry. Sadly, there was no time. The Austin-Healey Sprite (see Chapter Three) assuredly did for the Berkeley B95, the last of the line, in the same way that the Mini made life impossible for the bubble cars.

LIFE AFTER THE BUBBLE

Two British companies survived for years after the collapse of the bubble market, even though they were making odd little three-wheelers that owed their origins to the same kind of need. These survivors pushed the three arguable virtues of their products: first, that they were cheap to tax because of the three-wheeler concession;

As late as 1968, the designer of the Colliday Chariot was suggesting that the public might spend £300 (about half the price of a Mini) on this device which featured a 7-foot turning circle, two-pedal control – thanks to an automatic clutch – and a maximum speed of 'something over 30mph'. This may seem excessive, especially since the Chariot offered 'normal chair height seating' with a consequently high centre of gravity.

second, that they could be driven by anyone with a motor cycle licence without the need to take a car driving test; and third, that the grp bodies would never rust. These claims never stood up to serious scrutiny. In the first place, the saving on the annual road fund licence was minuscule by comparison with what you sacrificed by buying a low-volume, labour-intensive car which, in truth, cost a great deal in relation to what it offered (though it was true that, in some parts of the country, their resale value remained astonishingly high). As for the driving-licence concession, it only applied if the reverse gear was blanked off, and most of them weren't; in which case you were at risk of prosecution every time you drove without a proper car licence (but again, there seems to be no record of police stopping three-wheelers to check whether their reverse gears worked or not). As for the grp bodies, it was true they didn't rust. However, their metal attachments often did, and in any case, these early grp cars tended to degrade with time, and the body material collapsed into 'shredded wheat' if you suffered a serious bump.

It was true, though, that the three-wheelers were economical, for two very good reasons. One was that regulations insisted that the three-wheeler concession only applied if the car weighed less than 8cwt (406kg) in ready-to-drive condition – and lightness, as we have seen, is a great contributor to fuel economy. The second reason, though fiercely disputed by three-wheeler die-hards, was that the stability and handling

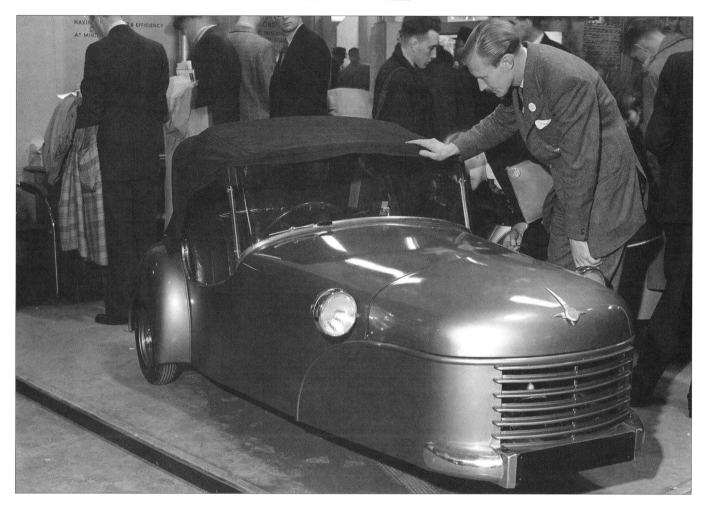

of these machines was so poor that nobody dared drive them consistently fast enough to use fuel at an enormous rate.

None of these truths put off a dedicated band of buyers who took two British companies to their hearts. One of these companies was Bond in Preston, Lancashire – founded by the same Laurie Bond who designed the Berkeley. For years, Bond made the 250, a device that resembled a grp bathtub into which four people could squeeze – father driving, mother alongside, and two (or, if small, even three) children on a hard and upright rear bench. The drive came from a 250cc motor-cycle engine – normally a Villiers – which not only drove the single front wheel via a chain drive, but actually turned with it when it steered, so that the steering felt shockingly heavy to anyone used to a normal car. The Bond 250, and the later, slightly smarter 250G sold remarkably well on its own doorstep, in the valley towns which had built around the already dying cotton industry. Its devoted following barely crossed the Pennines, and didn't extend all that far south, but on its own patch it was a familiar sight all the way through the 1960s. Some daring owners are known to have substituted much larger and more powerful motor-cycle engines for the original Villiers, at considerable cost in front-tyre and drive-chain life.

The launch of the original Bond Minicar at the 1949 Motor Cycle Show (three-wheelers were never considered 'proper' cars, and never allowed into the Motor Show). At the time, the Bond was billed as capable of 100mpg and 'upwards of 40mph', seating two in very modest comfort. The Bond evolved by stages (one of the last models is shown on the back cover) but like most similar machines, was condemned by the arrival of the Mini.

Bond made two attempts to break away from the 250 image while remaining faithful to the three-wheeler formula. The first involved a completely new design with a Hillman Imp engine, no less, driving the rear wheels, the single front wheel doing the steering as ever, with a compact, more-or-less four-seat grp body. With the featherweight aid of the all-aluminium Imp engine, this device, the Bond 875 (because the Imp engine was 875cc), just managed to creep beneath the 8cwt weight limit – making it around two-thirds the weight of the Imp itself – and was therefore remarkably fast, but preferably only in a straight line. It was in any case too expensive to prosper.

Bond's second 'breakaway' came after the company, having failed in an attempt to keep afloat by diversifying into Triumph Herald-based sports coupés, had already been taken over by its great three-wheeler rival, Reliant of Tamworth. The Bond Bug was an attempt to create a truly stylish three-wheeler – the shape came from the respected British consultancy of Ogle Design – and was a smooth wedge shape with a forward-hinged one-piece canopy. To add to the impact, for better or worse, you could only have it in bright orange. The Bug, however, was not really a Bond; all its important parts were Reliant. For all its twenty-first-century looks, in fact, under the wedge the Bug was just another Reliant Regal. The fact that, in order to meet the 8cwt limit, its size was so limited that the interior was too cramped to allow large people to drive it safely was almost incidental.

The company that took over Bond were Reliant of Tamworth, who had made three-wheelers in steadily increasing volume throughout the 1950s and into the 1960s. Reliant was unusual in making not only the cars but also the engines, developing a neat little four-cylinder, 750cc overhead-valve engine which was good enough to be accepted by the Austin Seven Owners' Club as a substitute for the 'real' 747cc Austin Seven power unit when these became difficult to obtain and very expensive. This engine was used to drive the rear wheels, leaving the front one to steer, and was fitted to a succession of grp-bodied three-wheeler designs which always managed, sometimes by ounces, to scrape under the 8cwt limit. The basic mechanical design never changed, only the body style. There was the Regal, then the Robin, and finally the Rialto – but the Robin is the one that caught the public imagination, even though most people today, for some inexplicable reason, refer to it as the Robin Reliant instead of the Reliant Robin. Where the Regal was angular, the Robin was smoother and had modern features like a top-hinged, opening rear window which made it into a mini-hatchback (through some miracle of weight saving, Reliant even offered a proper estate car version, too). Apart from the passenger versions, Reliant built commercial vans on the same chassis – and one of these vans, of course, found ultimate fame on television in the hands of Del Boy and the team.

Why have the Reliant three-wheelers hung on through thick and thin? To the honest and unbiased observer, they are cramped and nasty to drive, and by no means cheap. The secret seems to lie in the very 'three-wheeliness' of them. Ask a Robin owner why, and the first thing he (almost always he, almost always what the social scientists call a C2DE, a 'blue-collar' worker) will say is that the annual road fund licence is cheaper. There is still a kind of thrill in not handing over money to the government, even if it makes no economic sense: saving £50 by spending £500. The ultimate proof of this was created by Reliant itself. Twice the company made conventional four-wheeled adaptations of its three-wheelers: the Regal became the four-wheel Rebel and the Robin became the Kitten. The Kitten was certainly a much more desirable car than the Robin – there was more room in the cabin because the engine could go where the three-wheeler's front wheel sat, it was a lot quieter, and its stability and handling were of a completely different and superior order. Yet immediately, the comparison was not between the Robin and the Kitten but between the Kitten and the Mini – and the Mini was cheaper. The Robin you could not compare because, although it cost more than a Mini, it was a three-wheeler, wasn't it? And you save pounds a year on the road fund licence, you know . . . thus are motoring legends sometimes created, however undeservedly when seen from a coldly rational perspective.

One three-wheeler which just managed to survive the Mini onslaught was the Reliant Regal, which in turn sired the Robin and the high-style Rialto. It is not clear why the young lady should find the Regal so alluring, even if the car created a kind of cult following. Note the engine cover just ahead of the windscreen: the engine had to be that far back, since the single front wheel was installed ahead of it!

CHASING ECONOMY IN OTHER WAYS

The three-wheeler, however, is a strangely British aberration: the government could, if it wanted to, kill the tradition overnight by rewriting one tax regulation. Other countries also have their own strange ways of maintaining markets for distinctly odd cars. In France, for example, you are allowed to drive a very small car with an even smaller engine – governed so that it will not exceed 50kph (31mph) – without any kind of driving licence, and from the age of fourteen. These are the odd little 'scootacars', with names like Willum and Ligier, which one sees scuttling about the rural and small-town streets of middle France. And it is probably safer to allow fourteen-year-olds to become used to driving in something like this than to let them loose on motor cycles at the age of sixteen . . .

In Italy, there is a great tradition, though now apparently declining, of the Piaggio tricart. This is effectively the front half of a scooter mated with a two-wheel trailer, a simple axle beneath a tiny 'pick-up' container. While the Fiat 500 and 600 played their essential role in making Italy mobile, the Piaggio played no less important a part, the all-purpose, ultra-light commercial vehicle used for everything from taking vegetables to market to transporting amazing quantities of building materials, or almost anything else an artisan might need.

The Honda N360, and its larger-engined brother the N600, made a fairly determined foray into the British market in the mid-1960s. Despite the usual Japanese virtues of easy driving and reliability, their cramped interiors, high noise levels and poor ride comfort did not endear them to buyers, and this potential challenge to the Mini faded from the European scene.

The most elaborate market of all is the one created by the Japanese. Urban areas in Japan are so tightly packed that parking space is at a premium. Before you are allowed to buy a car, in fact, you must be able to show that you have an off-road parking place for it – unless it is a 'minicar'. The minicar is limited as to physical size (length and width), engine size (currently 660cc) and engine output (64hp). With the exception of Toyota and Nissan, all the Japanese manufacturers make minicars, and sell them in large numbers. Through the years, the regulations have been eased, partly because today's average Japanese is much bigger than the previous generation (the length and width limits have recently been eased yet again). The odd thing is that these small cars, to which a great deal of engineering effort is devoted, are almost impossible to sell anywhere else without substantial reworking.

In the 1960s, Honda decided it would import its then-current minicar, the N360 (at that time the maximum permitted engine size was 360cc). The company, rightly fearing that such an engine would be too small for British needs, also prepared a version with a substantially bigger engine, the N600: still only two-thirds the size of the Mini engine, but with roughly the same power output. When it was revealed that these cars were to be imported, there was a wailing and a gnashing of teeth in the popular British press, which predicted the Mini would soon be dead, swamped by this amazing little import. As we all know, the Mini did not die – and the Honda minicars eventually retired hurt, their lesson learned. Today, the Japanese engineer their smallest European cars in Europe, and the minicars mostly stay at home. Were the Japanese regulations to be eased rather more, of course . . . but industry experts have been saying that for thirty years already.

Back in the UK of the 1960s, the main British car manufacturers never even thought about making bubble cars, any more than Renault or Citroën did in France, or Volkswagen in Germany. The nearest they came to it were small conventional cars, successors to the pre-war 'eight horsepower' family runabouts before the market forgot all about the old RAC rating. So we had the Austin A30 and the Standard Eight, for example, but nothing smaller than that – until the advent of the Mini, which changed everything and banged nails into the bubble-car coffin almost as fast as they could be handed down. The odd thing is that unless you count the Imp, which was certainly designed as a Mini-competitor, nobody has ever made anything quite as compact as the Mini (at least, nobody has ever put such a design into production). It seems as though everyone looked at the Mini, admired it, and then convinced themselves they could make a much more appealing product if only they allowed it to be a foot longer and a couple of inches wider. Thus the most compact of rival cars, like the Fiat 127 and the Renault 5, have never quite been 'Mini'. That is probably inevitable: it isn't only the Japanese who are growing bigger, generation by generation. When the Mini was launched, it was a genuine four-seater, but few people would call it that today. Yet there are cars which are substantially more economical, in any given set of driving conditions, than the Mini has ever been. That is a measure of the technical progress which has been achieved in the second half of the twentieth century. The Mini has celebrated its fortieth birthday, after all . . .

CHAPTER SIX

SUPERCARS

*T*HERE IS A VERY LONG tradition of what we have come to call 'supercars' – extremely expensive cars with high performance, usually with stunning looks, built in small numbers for customers who can afford prices the average motorist can only dream about. It is the market in which Rolls-Royce, for example, has always operated. It is a very fickle market, strongly fashion-conscious and full of contradictions. For example, it has always been difficult for a volume car manufacturer, a Ford or Renault or Volkswagen, to convince the world it has produced a supercar, even when the specification and the care that has gone into its engineering suggest it has every right to be seen as one. Yet at times it has seemed quite easy for any entrepreneur with a well-equipped workshop, and sufficient wit to buy the rights to a once-famous old name, to design an extravagantly specified car, convince the market it is a supercar, and build the design in series in the expectation of selling at a substantial profit – substantial, because there is no upper end to the price range, and because part of the prestige of being a supercar owner is precisely because everyone knows the vehicle *is* hideously expensive.

Also, there are in effect two distinct supercar markets. Throughout the 1920s and 1930s the supercar concept split quite decisively. On the one hand there were the sports models, in which performance and impressive looks were the most important selling-points: the big Bentleys, the SSK Mercedes, the Bugattis, the Isotta-Fraschinis and Hispano-Suizas in Europe; and in the USA the Auburn, the Cord, the Duesenberg, the Pierce-Arrow and the Stutz among others. Then there were the ultimate luxury models, appealing to their well-heeled buyers on the strength of their comfort, space, refinement and sheer dominating presence: the Rolls-Royces of course, the larger Daimlers, the Bugatti Royale, the Delage, and in Germany the Horch and the Maybach as well as the big Mercedes saloons. In many cases, these

One of the best British interpretations of the 1960s supercar theme: the Aston Martin DB6, a classic car with an equally classic twin-cam, six-cylinder engine. The whole car was hand-assembled by craftsmen in the Aston Martin works at Newport Pagnell, still the home of the company in 1999, and still making many of its cars in the same tradition.

Considered by many to be a true supercar on a small scale, the original Ferrari Dino was powered by a mid-mounted V6 engine, and had a delicacy of behaviour to match its exquisite appearance. Later versions were more robust and practical, but could never quite lay claim to the esteem in which this car was held.

luxury carriages continued the tradition, established in the pioneering days when any kind of motor car was reserved for the rich, in which the customer took delivery of the chassis from Rolls-Royce (or whoever) and passed it to a coachbuilder who would clothe it with an elegant body to the customer's own design – or at least, to a design modified according to the customer's preferences.

Almost all these names vanished with the Second World War (some of them, after all, had been big engineering companies making small batches of prestige cars as a sideline, to keep workshops busy in idle times and to bolster the company image; Rolls-Royce itself had long been an aero-engine maker which also happened to make cars). In the USA, which might otherwise have kept the tradition going, all the small-volume 'prestige' manufacturers had either succumbed to financial troubles, or been absorbed into larger groups in which they lost their identities. Thus, after the war, of all those pre-war names, for a time only Rolls-Royce was left, and there were no sports supercars at all.

THE ITALIAN REBIRTH OF THE SPORTING SUPERCAR . . .

Then, in Italy, there began a new tradition led by Enzo Ferrari, who decided he could finance a winning Grand Prix team by making and selling a small (but sufficient) number of cars which would command a high price on the basis that they used the latest race-proved technology. For Ferrari, that crucially included V12 engines, similar – at least outwardly – to those which powered his early racing cars. Ferrari teams took part in both Grand Prix and competition sports-car racing, enjoying early and considerable success and building a reputation that meant his road-going sports cars were in great demand among those who could afford them.

Ferrari prospered – at least, he did until Grand Prix racing became a hugely expensive business, with race-car development costing far more than could be covered by the profits on a maximum of around 3,000 cars a year. For the sake of Italian national pride, the Ferrari concern was then absorbed into Fiat, which henceforth underwrote as much of the racing budget as could not be covered by sponsorship. But by that time, and on the strength of only a few thousand cars, Ferrari had re-established the tradition of the sporting supercar, and towards the end of the 1960s the company created perhaps the most famous of all, the Ferrari Daytona. A road test in *Autocar* magazine measured its maximum speed at 174mph, with acceleration to match.

Ferrari soon had his rivals. The earliest, from the same tradition but with a pre-war pedigree (Ferrari had worked for Lancia in the 1930s) were the brothers Maserati, his rival on the early post-war racetracks as well as on the road. Maserati road cars were not as technically advanced as their Ferrari rivals, especially in their chassis design and thus in the steering and handling, while their engines were six-cylinder or V8 rather than V12, but they always looked good. Maserati's last road car as an independent company was the beautiful Ghibli.

Perhaps the most astonishing aspect of the Italian supercar scene was the creation of Lamborghini, by a man who had made a lot of money building tractors, who loved fast cars and is supposed to have been infuriated when Enzo Ferrari failed to treat

The Ferrari 365GTB/4 Daytona laid claim for many years to being the fastest car whose maximum speed had been properly measured by an authoritative motoring magazine: 174mph was the magic figure. The front-engined, rear-driven Daytona was a formidable machine by any standards, with heavy controls which made it hard work to drive: but what rewards, if you had the skill and weren't afraid of the work!

Ferruccio Lamborghini was so upset by Enzo Ferrari's cavalier attitude to his customers that he revolted and designed his own car. His original attempt, the GT350 seen here, was a moderate success, beautiful in profile but ugly from any other direction (look at the tail treatment!). In the 1970s, however, Lamborghini was to reap his revenge in full with the sensational Miura.

him with the respect he thought he deserved. Starting with nothing but a bankroll and a burning desire to match Ferrari at his own game, Ferruccio Lamborghini created a small series of classic cars, with their own exquisite V12 engines, developed with the deliberate intention of upstaging Ferrari. Unlike Ferrari, Lamborghini never raced his cars (and neither did anyone else, at least, not seriously). His success was one of public relations: the fascinating story of the man who set out to make a better road car than Ferrari, and who may have succeeded.

Whether he really did remains a matter for debate. Of Lamborghini's cars the most famous, and the most beautiful, was the Miura, which appeared in 1966. The Miura was, in effect, the challenge to which the Daytona (first shown in 1968) was the response. Unlike the Daytona, the Miura was mid-engined, its V12 engine astonishingly installed across the car rather than in-line. This meant that despite its huge power, the car could be kept reasonably compact and the engine did nothing to interfere with the stunning styling. Which was the better of the two cars? There was little enough to choose between them in performance: the *Autocar* road test credited the Miura with a 170mph maximum against the Daytona's 174mph, but then the Ferrari engine was 4.4 litres as against the Lamborghini's 3.9 litres. But most drivers who have tried them both feel the Daytona was easier, as well as more rewarding to drive, partly because it was easier to see out of and therefore to place accurately on the road. It was the Miura, on the other hand, which turned every head in sight . . . sadly, the political upheavals and the 'energy crisis' looming just beyond the end of the 1960s dealt Lamborghini a blow from which it never fully recovered, although the company – passing through a succession of owners – managed to remain in being.

. . . AND A BRITISH RESPONSE

All this sporting-supercar activity in post-war Italy created an intense desire in some British hearts to do equally well, if not better. It wasn't easy, because the British post-war ethos was one of austerity, and because the British nation isn't as car-mad as Italy. 'In Italy,' as one British hero put it, 'when you corner at 100mph they shout *"Forza!"* ["Go for it!"], in Britain they shout "Madman!" '

The company that most seriously took up the challenge of creating a British supercar was Aston Martin, a pre-war builder of high-quality sports cars which, from 1948 onwards, steadily graduated to supercar status. Its post-war cars were the DB series, after its long-standing owner Sir David Brown, and they ran from DB2 to DB6 before switching from their traditional smooth design to the more angular lines of the DBS. Buyers in the 1960s had a choice of the standard coupé bodywork, or of the Volante convertible, and might order the Vantage engine with its extra power output – choices that continue to this day. In a tradition that paralleled Ferrari's, each Aston Martin engine was assembled by a single skilled technician, and the bodies were handcrafted before the cars were put together in a factory in Newport Pagnell in Buckinghamshire. Also like Ferrari, Aston Martin went racing, and man-

Aston Martin was a classic anyway, but the company established itself with a far wider audience when James Bond, in the form of Sean Connery, used a specially equipped DB5 (ejector seat, rotating multi-national number plates and sundry offensive devices) in the film Goldfinger. Those who could not afford the real thing (without the equipment) settled for the best-selling Corgi model.

aged to win the Le Mans Twenty-four-hours' race in 1959, beating the Ferraris in the process. Aston Martin actually made fewer cars even than Ferrari, and never a V12. For a long time its engines were large and magnificent six-cylinders, eventually replaced by an even bigger V8.

Alongside Aston Martin, Jaguar with its own mighty Le Mans tradition (winners of the race in 1951, 1953, 1955, 1956 and 1957) might have made it into the supercar class but for Sir William Lyons' obstinate insistence on making cars in sufficient numbers, and therefore sufficiently cheap, to be within conceivable reach of 'ordinary' motorists. No matter how good a car might be in every other respect, to qualify as a supercar its price had to place it beyond the reach of mere mortals. Sadly, Jaguar might have had a true supercar if things had worked out differently for the XJ13, a mid-engined – and extremely beautiful – giant with a V12 engine that was built in 1966 with the aim of achieving one more Le Mans victory for the company. But the XJ13 fell foul of the politics that bedevilled the British industry at the end of the 1960s, and of changes to the sporting regulations, and it was tucked away beneath dust-sheets for many years, before being revealed as a museum-piece. Today things are a little different, and the top sporting Jaguars – along with the Aston Martin DB7 and V8 – are regarded with the respect they fully deserve.

Was there anything to rival these Italian and British offerings? For the duration of the 1960s, there was nothing else of such quality. One French company, Facel Vega, made genuine supercars for a while (though with big American V8 engines) but it could not financially survive the 1960s despite a foray into the building of smaller, lighter cars that it hoped to sell in greater volume. It failed. As already mentioned,

To follow on from the DB series, Aston Martin introduced the more angular DBS, which began life with the same six-cylinder engine but was later powered by an all-new V8 capable of being Vantage-tuned to produce extremely high output. Although its lines were classic in every way, the nose shape of this early DBS reveals that aerodynamics had yet to be taken seriously in all departments.

the nearest thing to a supercar to emerge from France after that – to this day – was the Maserati-engined Citroën SM of 1970.

In Germany, meanwhile, the reborn motor industry was creeping towards the design and building of supercars. Both the Mercedes SL and the Porsche 911 began life as sports cars but quickly grew into supercars, adding engine size, power, weight and price, although it was the 1970s before they truly achieved this status. To pave the way for their ambitions, both companies became involved in racing during the 1950s. However, Mercedes, after two seasons (1954 and 1955) carrying all before them, suddenly stopped competing. True, 1955 had seen the awful crash of one of the works' SLRs at Le Mans, with the death of 80 spectators; but Mercedes managers admitted in later years that the racing programmes were soaking up engineering resources that they needed to develop their road-car range. Long before their regular production cars aspired to be supercars – that only came with the Mercedes 450SL and the Porsche 911 Turbo – both companies offered 'road-going' derivatives of their successful racing cars, Mercedes its famous 'gull wing' 300SL and Porsche with 'homologation' batches of various racing models.

By the mid-1960s, any car that could win at Le Mans was by definition a supercar of sorts. Winning might also be an excellent sales tool, an 'image booster' for any company. Ford thought along these lines and devoted immense effort to the develop-

A potential supercar which never progressed beyond its prototype stage was the Jaguar XJ13, developed with a view to repeating the company's Le Mans triumphs of the 1950s. Abandoned as too expensive and unlikely to be competitive by the time it was ready, the V12-engined XJ13 was later virtually destroyed in a high-speed test track accident, following tyre failure, only to be lovingly rebuilt by Jaguar apprentices to this state of perfection.

ment of a car that would win the race. The car emerged as the GT40, developed in and operated from the UK, which was already becoming the centre of the competition-car engineering world. The GT40 was a smooth mid-engined machine, as efficient as it was good-looking, and it duly won Le Mans every year from 1966 to 1969. Did it do Ford's image any good? Yes, undoubtedly. Did the GT40 achieve success as a road-going supercar? Not really, although a good many were made and finished in road-car trim. Two things had happened. The pace of development meant that cars which could win races like Le Mans simply were no longer practical for everyday use on normal roads: not enough ground clearance, too noisy, too cramped inside, and very hard work to drive in traffic. That apart, as became clear, the name Ford simply wasn't right for a supercar. For the ultra-rich buyer, the image and the tradition were everything. Better an obscure foreign name that meant little to anyone, than the all-too familiar badge of a company which made family cars by the hundred thousand.

Top **Vertically paired headlamps were a prominent feature of the Facel Vega, the only post-war French supercar. Although made in some numbers and admired by many, the Facel could not survive the French government's attitude to fast, heavy, thirsty cars.**

Above **The Mercedes 190SL was the company's first post-war sports car. While it could hardly be considered a supercar, its larger-engined stablemate the 300SL certainly had ambitions in that direction, especially in its famous 'gull-wing' form with upward opening doors.**

Opposite **The Bristol, made in an aircraft factory, was always a car for the discerning. This early model retained the company's efficient 2-litre engine of German origin; later versions used American V8 power.**

CHEAP POWER, AND LOTS OF IT

The lesson was not lost on those entrepreneurs who wanted to try their luck in the potentially lucrative supercar market. You needed a car with looks and performance, yes. You needed the right kind of name, something with an exotic ring to it. But did you need a Ferrari, a Lamborghini, a Maserati or an Aston Martin, with an expensive engine individually assembled by craftsmen, or could you offer fearsome performance without going to the equally fearsome expense of designing and building your own power unit? The example of Facel Vega suggested you could. The alternative approach adopted by this company was to import a large American V8 engine, not by any means as powerful as a Ferrari V12 but inherently reliable, with its own exciting noise, and with the additional advantage of coming complete with a well developed automatic transmission (by the 1960s, less than half of supercar customers wanted to undertake the hard work of exercising a clutch pedal and shifting their own gears). The only question was whether rich enthusiasts would accept this hybrid Euro-American formula. The answer was that some wouldn't, but quite a few would, as long as the looks and the performance were right.

Among the better known cars to adopt the 'American V8' formula were Bristol, Gordon-Keeble and Jensen in the UK, and in Italy, de Tomaso in the Mangusta and Pantera, and Iso in the Grifo and the Rivolta. The favourite engine for the purpose was a Chrysler V8, an immensely tough unit that could be tuned to provide a lot of

power if needed. It was used by Bristol and by Jensen, and also by a small Swiss manufacturer, Monteverdi, who for some time made cars in very small numbers to the same general formula. Bristol chose their engine with great care, and used it to replace a 2-litre, six-cylinder unit (with its origins in pre-war BMWs) in their cars from the 407 onwards to achieve a huge boost in performance. Jensen used Chrysler V8 power in the grp-bodied 541, and then in the boldly styled, metal-bodied Interceptor, and in the longer-bodied FF, which pioneered the use of four-wheel drive in a road car as opposed to an off-road vehicle like the Jeep or Land Rover. The FF was an altogether remarkable car in its way – it also pioneered the use of anti-lock brakes, using a Dunlop Maxaret system taken straight from an aircraft – and Jensen survived through the 1960s, although it encountered problems later, like so many of the 1960s supercar makers. De Tomaso and Iso used Ford V8 engines and, for a while, de Tomaso turned this to advantage by selling a remarkable number of Panteras in the USA, promising service from friendly local Ford dealers. None of these companies made cars in huge numbers, except for the considerable de Tomaso total, but the names still resonate with enthusiasts.

It must be said, however, that some of these cars were underdeveloped and suffered from serious faults. In 1969, the respected American magazine *Road and Track* called the de Tomaso Mangusta 'without a doubt, the most beautiful car in series production'. But it concluded its road test of the car by asking 'How much driving enjoyment can you get from a sports car that has tricky handling, mediocre brakes and terrible shift linkage?' To this you could all too often add a heating and ventila-

Jensen cars of West Bromwich spent the 1980s producing the Chrysler V8-powered Interceptor and its pioneer 4WD derivative, the FF (Ferguson Formula). This is an FF, identified by two (rather than just one) side grilles in the front wing, disguising the extra length needed for the 4WD transfer gearbox. The massive, top-opening rear hatch was another very modern feature in this era.

tion system, and a control layout, which had obviously been designed after the engineering team had run out of time and enthusiasm. In the British market, some of the things done to convert small-volume supercars to right-hand drive beggared belief, and should never have been allowed: the *Autocar* road-test team experienced two mechanical 'crossover' failures in supercars converted to right-hand drive, either of which – given bad luck – would have been potentially fatal. This, rather than the choice of engine, was what made the difference between the pretenders and the true thoroughbreds like Ferrari and Aston Martin.

However, perhaps the most famous application of an American engine, and one which was certainly very well engineered, was made by an American, Carroll Shelby, who took a medium-sized sports car made by AC, a tiny but long-established company in south-west London (a company that made most of its profits building motor-

ized invalid carriages for the Ministry of Health) and 'shoehorned' beneath its bonnet the Ford '427' (meaning a 427cu in displacement, or 7-litre) V8. The result was the Shelby Cobra, which a lot of enthusiasts still consider the ultimate in sheer blood-tingling, road-going 'brutality'. If the '427' was too much for you, there was an alternative '289', a mere 4.7 litres. The British AC company itself had little to do with this development, but was building, in extremely small numbers, its own interpretation of the supercar, the AC428, powered by the same big Ford V8 engine.

A SUBTLE SHIFT OF EMPHASIS

It was during the 1960s that the market for sporting supercars underwent a subtle shift. Up to that time, in most of Europe outside built-up areas, cars were allowed to drive as fast as the driver wished, up to the maximum of which they were capable. In the case of the supercars, as we have seen, this could be up to 170mph or more.

There were not, of course, many places where this could be done in safety – even fewer than now, because the building of today's motorway network had barely begun, except in West Germany and Italy. In any event, as the 1960s wore on, speed limits began to spread wider. The UK brought in its universal 70mph limit, and there was a European trend towards some kind of limit, often 130kph (81mph). Was this to spell the end of the supercar? Apparently not. It merely underlined the fact that many owners bought them, as the British would say, for show rather than for go. It was still essential that the car should be very fast indeed, although it was some time before any production car could reliably exceed the Daytona's 174mph, but this was to enable the owner to tell people how fast it would go, rather than actually to try it himself (even today, 95 per cent of supercar owners and drivers are men, possibly because women are more sensible).

General Motors decided during the 1950s that it did dare to produce a sports car, so long as the effort did not interfere too much with its mainstream activities. The result was the plastic-bodied Chevrolet Corvette, seen here it is innocuous-looking original incarnation, but already with formidable performance. Once it was established and admired, generations of GM stylists sought to move the Corvette towards the twenty-first century. They are still trying . . .

Speed limits had astonishingly little effect on the way supercars were designed from the 1960s onwards, although the political and fuel-supply problems of the next decade certainly shrank the market and put a number of companies out of the business altogether. Sometimes it was argued that 'you could still go to Germany and drive as fast as you wished' (this was usually said by people who had little current experience of driving on crowded German *autobahns* with their frequent roadworks). It was even argued that people who were rich enough to buy supercars were rich enough to hire racetracks for their ultimate driving enjoyment, a suggestion that poses more questions than it answers about the reasons why people buy such cars.

What did happen was that the makers of high-performance cars lower down the social ladder changed direction. The conventional sports car, as we saw in Chapter Three, fell out of fashion. There was far greater emphasis on cars that accelerated well and would go round corners quickly, and which would be essentially comfortable and practical, without offering the all-out maximum speed of the supercar. The 'hot hatch' had arrived, but the supercar owner would never dream of venturing out

The epitome of British elegance and top-level craftsmanship: and for a while, during the 1960s, the engineering caught up in this car, the Silver Shadow. Unitary body, disc brakes, independent rear suspension: by Rolls-Royce standards, it was a technical revolution. But to the customer, the leather, the wood, and the gloss of the 20-coat paint finish were what really mattered – along with the respect of policemen and top hotel commissionaires.

in one, unless he wanted to avoid recognition and experience the strange sensation of *not* being stared at.

Much later, there was a brief period of madness in which the 'classic' supercars, especially those of the 1960s, became the subject of a collectors' market, which turned by stages into an investors' market. The word was that a safe and profitable way of investing money was to buy a 'classic' car, because the value of such cars could only keep rising. Thirty-year-old Ferraris in particular, and some other models, began to change hands for the most alarming – not to say silly – prices. Eventually, and inevitably, the market collapsed. Some people who had bought at its peak suffered financially, while those who had sold at its peak chuckled all the way to the bank. It provided a salutary lesson in the need to see any car, even a supercar, for what it is. Ferraris are not Picassos.

A MORE STATELY WORLD

Meanwhile, what was happening in the rarefied world of the top-level saloon car? Life was by no means as exciting here as it was among the sporting supercars. There was much less competition. It was not that the market was smaller, more that customers applied a different set of values, much more difficult to approach in engineering terms. It was much easier (and, it must be said, more fun) to build a fast, exciting and very expensive car than to build a comfortable, dignified and very expensive one. In the immediate post-war era, it might have been said that only one surviving company knew exactly how to do it, and that was Rolls-Royce. The company continued, because Rolls-Royce had always existed, and not even a devoutly socialist post-war British government had the nerve to force it to close (Britain needed the export earnings, however much such symbols of opulence offended some people).

Rolls-Royce, with its car factory now at Crewe, remained faithful to the traditions of its founder Sir Henry Royce (C. S. Rolls, his non-engineering partner, was killed in a flying accident in 1910, and at best probably only saw two or three of the firm's earliest cars). Sir Henry, who survived until 1933, would never allow new technology into his cars until it had been honed to perfection and proved utterly reliable, a process that could take many years. As a result, in 1960 the beautifully made and supremely elegant Silver Cloud remained, beneath its skin, a 1930s car, hopelessly out of date by any normal standard. To a certain kind of customer, naturally, that mattered much less than the status conferred by the world's best-known radiator grille and the 'flying lady' mascot. Those who remained faithful to the Bentley name, owned by Rolls-Royce since the 1930s, were becoming ever more incensed at the way their favourite was being made to play second fiddle in the market. The 1960s were probably the nadir for Bentley, which emerged as little more than a badge-engineered, slightly cheaper Rolls-Royce. Things improved for Bentley later on . . . but in the meantime, even Rolls-Royce had some major surprises up its sleeve for the mid-1960s.

Overleaf *If you had real money and were in a position to consider the Silver Shadow almost mass-produced, Rolls-Royce would instead offer you the Corniche convertible, with massive folding hood (power operated, naturally) and an interior which was the height of luxury. Needless to say, the Corniche was built in very small numbers, thus achieving instant classic status – more so, in fact, than the Pininfarina-styled Camargue which had been intended as the topmost Rolls-Royce.*

Having first discarded its clumsy old six-cylinder engine in favour of a big (6.2-litre) V8, which might almost have been American but for the expensive care lavished on its production and assembly, Rolls-Royce proceeded to astonish the world in 1965 with its introduction of the Silver Shadow. This was an almost shockingly new car, certainly by Rolls-Royce standards. Gone was the trusty chassis frame, replaced by a unitary bodyshell. Gone was the live rear axle (one has the impression that not too many years before, Rolls-Royce had been reluctant even to embrace independent front suspension) to be replaced by independent rear suspension with semi-trailing arms. Gone were the huge and heavy drum brakes, replaced by discs on all four wheels. Even before the Shadow, the Silver Cloud had been fitted with a 'standard' steel body – the coachbuilding trade was in decline – but in engineering terms the new car was definitely revolutionary, and a huge programme by previous Rolls-Royce standards. Under the pressure, some surprising details were overlooked: almost to the last moment, it was intended to call the new car the Silver Mist – until somebody looked in a German dictionary and discovered that all good German farmyards kept a heap of *mist* in one corner, ready for spreading (this is by no means the only motor industry example of disastrous misnaming, and some of them have reached production!).

The original Silver Shadow, and its badge-engineered equivalent the Bentley T, were good, but not without their faults. To begin with, in particular, they were supremely comfortable, but they were not all that pleasant to drive. Ten years previously, that wouldn't have mattered so much, for no Rolls-Royce owner would have dreamed of driving himself (Bentley owners were always a slightly different matter). As it was, the company began a development programme in which the chassis was modified, by degrees, until eventually the Silver Shadow was much nicer to drive – but never fun. Alongside the Silver Shadow and the Bentley T series, two even more expensive models kept alive the last vestiges of the coachbuilding tradition: the Rolls-Royce Corniche (with its companion the Bentley Continental) and the huge Phantom V, a car very much for arrivals in state.

In the USA, the top-line cars from the three major manufacturers, the Imperial (from Chrysler), the Lincoln (from Ford) and the Cadillac Fleetwood (from General Motors) were already so huge, so luxuriously equipped and so powerful that there seemed little point in anyone setting out to build anything even bigger and better – so nobody did; except that individuals remained free to have workshops 'stretch' their Cadillacs (it seems mainly to have been Cadillacs) by a few feet to create a car in which you could hold a business meeting or a small party. That left the 'exclusive' US market to Rolls-Royce – until the Germans decided to compete, in the shape of Mercedes.

Before the Second World War, Mercedes had built a whole series of impressive cars, but the most impressive of all had been the Grosser Mercedes, a giant with a 7.7-litre straight-eight engine. Throughout the 1950s Mercedes worked to re-establish

The 1960s saw Mercedes launch a bid to take over Rolls-Royce territory with the huge 600, a monster car powered by a 6.3-litre V8 engine. As this Swiss-registered example shows, the 600 was certainly impressive; but it could never be subtly understated in the manner which Rolls-Royce had made its own. For leaders of government and captains of industry, it was simply a question of which approach you preferred.

itself, moving steadily up the market, and then in 1964 it launched its new Grosser Mercedes, the 600, powered by a 6.3-litre V8 engine. It seemed clear that the 600 was a deliberate attempt not only to regain the heights of pre-war prestige but also to outdo Rolls-Royce, even to the fact that the 600 engine was marginally bigger. Even this was not sufficient for the German company, which later offered a further stretched version, the 600 Pullman. While relatively few customers, in Europe at least, actually bought the 600 it had a powerful effect on the Mercedes image, and remained in production for some time. Most of Mercedes' top-level customers were actually content with the slightly smaller S-class cars, clearly content that it didn't matter if the same three-pointed star emblem adorned the bonnets of half the world's taxis. Of the other German manufacturers, BMW didn't really get into the prestige act, with its 7 series, until much later, while Audi left it later still.

In France and Italy, the potential market was much too small for anyone to think of starting to build prestige supercars. When transport for the top brass was needed, it was specially adapted (rather as in the USA) by a specialist who would lengthen a standard model – usually a Citroën DS in France, a Lancia or possibly an Alfa Romeo in Italy – and fit it with a special roof, calling the result 'Présidentiel' in France, or 'Ministeriale' in Italy. Some of the Italian sports-supercar manufacturers toyed with the idea of stretching their cars into low-slung four-door saloons (as did Aston Martin in the UK, in a revival of the Lagonda name). The most persistent of these offerings came from Maserati with its Quattroporte – literally, four-door; but it failed to make any real impact, in Italy or overseas. Ferrari never contemplated making a four-door model, even for a moment. Its sporting heritage was far too important to risk spoiling in that way.

So, by the end of the 1960s, if you wanted a top car to be chauffeured around in, your choice still lay between a Rolls-Royce and a Mercedes, or a Daimler at a pinch (remember, the British Royal Family remained faithful to Daimler for many years). If you were American, there was always the option of a 'stretch Caddy'. If you wanted exotic excitement the choice was much wider, with Ferrari, Lamborghini and Maserati all competing hard, plus Aston Martin, Bristol or Jensen if you wanted to stay British, or the top Mercedes or Porsche.

Among the sporting cars, after the 1960s had ended, most of the manufacturers passed through hard times and some barely survived. Ferrari remained supreme in Italy, Mercedes and Porsche continued on their efficient way in Germany – although, for some enthusiasts, they build too many examples even of their top-range cars for them to be seen as supercars. In the UK, Aston Martin prospers and the latest Jaguars meet the most demanding requirements. Even little TVR has steadily climbed the ladder of prestige, building small numbers of cars with its own advanced V8 and V12 engines, supercars in the making.

As for the 'limousine supercars', it became ever clearer as time went on that the battle for supremacy lay between Rolls-Royce and the biggest Mercedes, although for many of the people who mattered the Rolls-Royce always had the edge because Mercedes could never quite shake off that 'Stuttgart taxi' image, for all its technical efficiency. Others tried to challenge this dual supremacy but always fell well short in one respect or another. The big problem for Rolls-Royce was that time was running out: the company (and even its parent company, Vickers) was too small to bear the enormous cost of developing a completely new car, a replacement for the Silver Shadow and its later derivatives, to meet all the safety and emissions regulations now in force. As we now know, the sad resolution of the situation was that the Volkswagen group bought Rolls-Royce. Yet in a way this was the greatest vindication of all, a classic illustration of 'if you can't beat them, join them'. And the UK has the reassurance that Rolls-Royce standards, and the Rolls-Royce image, will most assuredly be maintained.

As for the British industry as a whole, as we pointed out in Chapter Two, the 1960s were a kind of 'golden age' – but shortly to be followed by a much darker one. There was already a problem with the sprawling mass of British Leyland (BL) – essentially a merger between BMC and Leyland-Standard-Triumph, with Rover and Jaguar-Daimler thrown in for good measure. It was a group building dozens of different models in uneconomic numbers in a score of factories, some of them small and ill-equipped. An exceptionally strong management might have taken the situation by the scruff of the neck, pruned the product range to something more rational – all too many of BL's products competed with each other – closed factories where necessary and expanded others. Sadly, that kind of management was lacking, to the extent where BL quickly sank into a financial mire from which nationalization, unthinkable today, seemed the only way out. It is easy to blame the management of BL for everything that happened, but the British government bore a good deal of the blame. In 1969 the British car market was hamstrung by restrictions, especially on hire purchase. You had to pay one-third of the cost immediately, and the balance in a fairly short time. Early in the 1970s, all those restrictions were swept away, and the car market boomed. Unfortunately, British factories, and especially BL, were poorly placed to expand production and most of the benefit went to imported cars.

With the benefit of hindsight, it is easy to see that if British manufacturers had paid more attention to what was happening abroad, they might have been better placed to fight off these foreign buyers. They might have had better products and better product quality. Instead, the 1960s was a decade in which the British industry lived by the slogan 'we know what's best for our own market'. Some of the industry's achievements were among the best, from the Mini to the Rover 2000, the Jaguar E-type, the Aston Martin DBS and the Rolls-Royce Silver Shadow. But as the decade wore on, the innovative brilliance of the engineers who created these cars was more and more overshadowed by the doubts of accountants to whom caution was everything, and who starved the industry of the long-term investment it needed to create the next generation of world-class designs. Twenty years later, the necessary investment in the British industry had at last been made – but not by British companies. Ford and Vauxhall were 'inward investments' of long standing; by the 1990s they were to be joined by BMW, Honda, Nissan, Peugeot, Toyota and Volkswagen, leaving Morgan and TVR vying for the title of largest wholly British-owned car manufacturer. The consolation is that Britain at the end of the century builds almost twice as many cars as it did a decade ago – and builds them better, and in great variety. Unlike 1969, the view ahead from 1999 looks promising.

SELECTED BIBLIOGRAPHY

Autocar Road Test Yearbooks, 1960–1970 (Iliffe, London, published bi-annually)

Pat Braden and Gerald Roush, *The Ferrari 365 GTB/4 Daytona* (Osprey, London, 1982)

Richard Crump and Bob de la Rive Box, *Maserati Road Cars* (Osprey, London, 1979)

J. R. Daniels, *British Leyland – The Truth About the Cars* (Osprey, London, 1980)

J. R. Daniels, *Citroën SM* (Osprey, London, 1981)

Pierre Dumont, *Citroën: Quai de Javel – Quai André Citroën* (editions E.P.A., Paris, 1977)

Eric Dymock, *The Jaguar File* (Dove Publishing, Sutton Veny, 1998)

Eric Dymock, *The Renault File* (Dove Publishing, Sutton Veny, 1998)

Paul Frère, *Porsche 911 Story* (Patrick Stephens, Cambridge, 3rd edition 1984)

Rob Golding, *Mini* (Osprey, London, 1979)

Ray Hutton, *Sports Cars* (Hamlyn, London, 1973)

Brian Long, *The Marques of Coventry* (Wheaton, Exeter, 1990)

Pete Lyons, *The Complete Book of Lamborghini* (Haynes, Yeovil, 1988)

F. Wilson McComb, *Aston Martin V8s* (Osprey, London, 1981, and 2nd edition, 1984)

F. Wilson McComb, *MG* (Osprey, London, 1971, and 2nd edition, 1978)

Motor Road Test Yearbooks, 1960–1970 (Temple Press, London, published annually)

Motor Yearbooks, 1950–1957 (Temple Press, London, published annually)

Motoring Which? Yearbooks, Volumes 1–7 (Consumers' Association, London, published annually)

Jan P. Norbye, *BMW* (Publications International, Skokie, Illinois, USA, 1984)

Jan P. Norbye, *De Tomaso Pantera* (Osprey, London, 1982)

Jon Pressnell, *Great Cars of the World* (Prion, London, 1992)

Peter Roberts, *A Pictorial History of the Motor Car* (F&S Pubications, New York, 1977)

Graham Robson, *Fiat Sports Cars from 1945 to the X1/9* (Osprey, London, 1984)

Graham Robson, *The Rolls–Royce and Bentley, Volume 3, Shadow, Corniche, Camargue* (Motor Racing Publications, London, 1985)

Society of Motor Manufacturers and Traders, *The Motor Industry of Great Britain* (London; published annually)

Dick Stirley and Keith Read, *MIRA – 50 Years of Excellence* (Motor Industry Research Association, Nuneaton, 1996)

David G. Styles, *Alfa Romeo – The Legend Revived* (Dalton Watson, London, 1985)

The Car (Orbis, London: partwork 1983–85)

Ian Ward, *Lotus Elan – Coupé, Convertible, Plus 2* (Osprey, London, 1984)

Ian Webb, *Ferrari Dino 206GT, 246GT and GTS* (Osprey, London, 1984)

Jonathan Wood, *The Motor Industry of Great Britain Centenary Book* (Society of Motor Manufacturers and Traders, London, 1996)

Andrew Whyte, *Aston Martin and Lagonda, Volume 1* (Patrick Stephens, Wellingborough, 1980 and 2nd edition, 1984)

Andrew Whyte, *Jaguar* (Patrick Stephens, Wellingborough, 1980 and 2nd edition, 1985)

INDEX

(Numbers in **bold** refer to illustrations)

Picture Acknowledgements

a = above, b = below, l = left, r = right, c = centre

British Leyland: 65; British Motor Industry Heritage Trust:10, 20, 35, 36, 38, 48; Neill Bruce: 42, 80, 83a, 104, 114, 118 & 122, 22-23, 67a, 93, 120, 121b, 124, & 130 (Peter Roberts Collection), 82a (The Midland Motor Museum Bridgnorth); Corbis:19, 39, 50, 52 & 119a (Hulton-Deutsch Collection), 60, 63 (Nik Wheeler), 141 (Bettmann), 143 (Vince Streano), 139 (Chris Taylor, Cordaiy Library Ltd); Ronald Grant Archive/Eon Productions: 137; Crispin Eurich:55b; Hulton Getty:127; National Motor Museum Beaulieu:24, 27, 28, 31, 32, 40, 41, 44, 55a, 58, 59, 64, 68, 69, 76, 78 79, 81, 82b, 84, 85, 87, 89, 92, 98, 100, 101, 102b, 106b, 107, 112, 117, 119b, 123, 125, 129, 134, 135, 136, 140a & b, 142, 145, & 149, 121a (Georgano), 66, 77, 83b, 103, 108, 110 & 111, (Rover Group/BMIHT/Beaulieu), 54, 56-57, 62, 74 & 106a(N.Wright); Penguin Books Ltd: 118a; Topham Picturepoint:12, 13, 47a & b & 126; Reproduced by kind permission of Vintage Ad Gallery:71, 88a & b, 90, 96, 97, 102a, 105, 109a & b